PINK SLIP PROOF

-how to control all future paychecks

Foreword by Tom Hopkins
Professional Sales Trainer, Speaker, and Author

Paul J. Meyer

New York Times Best-Selling Author

Pink Slip PROOF ... *how to control all future paychecks*

Published by Sales and Service Excellence,
a division of Executive Excellence Publishing
1806 N. 1120 W. Provo, UT 84604
www.leaderexcel.com

Printed in the United States of America

ISBN 978-0-9791957-9-2
BUSINESS & ECONOMICS / Sales & Selling

TO GET YOUR ATTENTION ...

Let's start with the money that can be made in selling. Over Paul J. Meyer's lifetime sales career, his income:
- Has annually averaged over $8 million
- In today's dollars, that is over one billion dollars of personal income

The number of companies started by Paul J. Meyer:
- Over 100 (started)
- Over 40 (active and profitable today) spread around the world

How much money was originally invested into his first company:
- Just $1,000 in 1960

Paul's family's charitable foundations:
- The Paul and Jane Meyer Family Foundation, started less than 20 years ago, has donated over $65 million mostly to central Texas charities and ministries.

Paul J. Meyer has received the following honorary degrees:
- Honorary Doctorate of Aviation Education Degree, Embry-Riddle Aeronautical University, 1971
- Honorary Doctorate of Humane Letters Degree, Fort Lauderdale University, 1971
- Honorary Doctorate of Letters Degree, East Texas Baptist University, 1989
- Honorary Doctorate of Humane Letters Degree, Central Penn College, 2007
- Honorary Doctorate of Humanities Degree, Mary Hardin-Baylor University, 2007

Paul J. Meyer has received the following other honors:
- Baylor University:

- Alumni by Choice, 1987
- Alumnus Honoris Causa
- James Huckins Award
- Pat Neff Award
- Paul J. Meyer Arena in Ferrell Special Events Center named in his honor, 1988
- President's Medal, 1988
- W.R. White Meritorious Service Award, 1988
- Golden Key National Honor Society, 1992

- Boy Scouts of America:
  - Distinguished Eagle Scout Award, 1983 (very few people have ever received this award)
  - Distinguished Citizen Award, Heart O' Texas Council, 1987
  - Silver Keystone Award, 1987
  - Scouting: Good Shepherd Emblem, 1992
  - James E. West Fellowship Award, Heart O' Texas Council, 1994
  - The Founders Award, Heart O' Texas Council, 1994

- Achievement Award, Success Club of Great Britain
- Honorary Vice-President, Sales Executives Club of South Africa
- National Sales Leadership Award, Houston Sales Executive Club
- Freedoms Foundation Award, 1983, Valley Forge, PA
- Americanism Award, Houston Jaycees (same year as Art Linkletter)
- Boys & Girls Clubs of Waco Mom & Dad for a Year, 1991
- Boys Club of America Medallion for Outstanding Service
- Investor Hall of Fame for Investment Excellence, 1992
- Haggai Institute for Advanced Leadership, Distinguished Founder's Award, Singapore, 1990
- Paul J. Meyer Day, Waco, Texas, June 17, 1969
- Paul J. Meyer Day, Waco, Texas, September 17, 1987

- Philanthropist of the Year, Central Texas Chapter of Fundraising Professionals, 2001
- Small Business Person of the Year Award, Waco Chamber of Commerce, 1988
- Plus 100 similar awards

An abbreviated summary of Paul's career:

1948 - 1957:
Mastering Selling

Insurance Sales – Began insurance career immediately after military service and quickly became a top producer, leading two of the nation's largest life insurance companies. By age 27, acquired a personal net worth of $1,000,000 (worth $12,000,000 in today's dollars) from personal production and agency development.

1958 - 1959:
Preparing to Launch My Dream Company

Sales Executive with a Waco, Texas, firm distributing religious books and records. Increased its business 1,500% in 24 months. My purpose of working for the company was to learn all about the audio recording business.

1960 - present:
Launching and Growing 40+ Companies

Founded Success Motivation® Institute, Inc., (now Success Motivation® International, Inc.) and shortly thereafter **Leadership Management®, Inc. and Leadership Management International, Inc.** These firms were established for the purpose of helping people develop their full potential, plus leadership skills.

- The product line of these companies has expanded to include over **40 full-length courses** and programs on attitude, goal setting, motivation, leadership development, and time managment.

- These programs and courses are marketed in more than **60 countries** of the free world and are produced in **26 languages** with others in preparation.

- Combined sales are approaching **$3 billion worldwide**, establishing Paul J. Meyer **as the preeminent leader** in the self-improvement industry.

Along with being considered by many to be the founder of the present self-improvement industry and the above-mentioned companies, Paul and his family's companies are in auto racing, computers, legal insurance, aircraft sales, real estate development, printing, publishing, product development, nutrition, and more.

- Royalties and overrides from his program sales are in the **hundreds of millions**, but when combined with commissions and profits from his other business ventures, his lifetime personal earnings are over $1 billion (in today's dollars).

And it's a given ... there will be more companies in the future, more money earned, and more to give away, all because he chose to master selling.

I have come to believe this:

SELLING is

unequivocally,

indisputably,

undeniably,

irrefutably,

obviously,

definitely,

plainly,

and without question

THE WORLD'S
GREATEST OPPORTUNITY!

**It is how you
Pink Slip PROOF yourself!**

CONSIDER THIS!

by Paul J. Meyer

The sky is the limit!

There is no limit to what you can do or become when you choose selling, the world's greatest profession.

You will accomplish great things as a salesperson, and you will become a greater person as a result!

Take it to the bank!

This book was not written from a research point of view or an academic point of view. It was written from a practical hands-on, in-the-trenches, been-there-done-that point of view.

You can trust what I'm saying because I've lived it, breathed it, and done it.

I once entered a competition that offered a special watch if you could make 60 sales in 60 days … and asked if I could change the rules.

Brazenly, I told the owner of the company, "Sixty sales in 60 days is too easy. **I'll do 60 sales in a row!**"

He gave me permission, no doubt thinking that I had a few screws loose somewhere.

I went out and I did it!

Sixty consecutive sales later, in a matter of four short days, I won my watch. I didn't need the watch. I just wanted to do it. Over the years, I have made tens of millions of dollars again and again by honing and developing my skills until I became a master salesman. I'm still learning every day.

Millions served

I have had the pleasure of having millions — *literally* — of customers over the past 60+ years. I didn't personally sell to a million people, but every customer who has used one of my programs has created a bond with me … because I genuinely believe they get *"a piece of me"* when they use my programs. Thank you all!

You can do it!

Allow the words of this book to challenge you, encourage you, motivate you, and open your eyes to the limitless possibilities that only salespeople can enjoy.

CONTENTS

FOREWORD

by Tom Hopkins

Without question, Paul J. Meyer is one of the best salesmen of all time. I've been involved in the profession of selling and sales training since the 1960's myself and have been inspired by Paul's success all of my business life.

Many folks have even said that he is THE single greatest salesman, ever. They could be right. Paul J. Meyer has never been second. Not once! In every company he has ever sold for and every sales competition he has ever entered, he led them all and won them all.

The late W. Clement Stone, founder of Combined Insurance Company and author of one of the best-selling motivational books of all time, *Success Through a Positive Mental Attitude*, said: "Paul J. Meyer is the greatest salesman who ever wore shoe leather."

Charlie Becker, President of Franklin Life Insurance Company believes: "Paul's sales records will never be broken."

What do I think? I believe Paul J. Meyer to be the Tiger Woods of selling — a true sales legend. Fewer than a handful of people are even in his league.

Paul started selling at age 12 and won a national competition for selling *Ladies Home Journal* and *Liberty Magazine*.

At age 14, he sold local farmers on giving him the exclusive right to pick all their fruit for 25 cents a box. He turned around and hired a whole army of workers to get the job done, paying them 20 cents a box each. Now, there's entrepreneurial spirit for you!

His earnings by age 15 exceeded that of most adults by the tune of 400%. He had saved more money by the age of 16 than the combined savings of every child and adult he knew.

After high school, Paul enlisted in the United States Paratroopers. He made a deal with his colonel not to be shipped overseas if he could break the U.S. military fitness records. He did break the fitness records of the day and stayed stateside as a physical fitness instructor.

When World War II ended, Paul entered the insurance industry. By the age of 25, Paul had accomplished more than most men who had been in the business twice as long. His accomplishments included:

- leading the largest exclusive *weekly premium* insurance company
- leading the largest exclusive *ordinary* insurance company in the nation
- building one of the largest life insurance agencies in America
- being the youngest member of the Million Dollar Round Table, and
- being the highest paid insurance person in America

Who wouldn't want to learn from and work for a man like this? Paul traveled the world over and has recruited a sales force from every major city on every continent. His powerful training programs are indeed life changing. Suffice it to say, Paul speaks from experience, and now offers that experience to you as an author of unparalleled credibility.

This book is an incredible resource for anyone in the profession of selling. Keep in mind, though, that it's not about "how to sell." Rather, it's about the incredible profession of selling … the benefits, the freedom, and financial rewards that only a career in selling can provide for you and your loved ones.

If you're already in selling, this is a book you should read at least once every year to remind you why you chose selling as a career.

If you're thinking about selling as a career, if this book doesn't persuade you of the wonderful life it can bring to you, nothing will.

If you are a business owner or manager of a sales team, let me suggest you use this book to recruit an army of people into the world's greatest profession — selling!

The famous novelist and poet Robert Louis Stevenson once said, "Everyone lives by selling something." Why not make it a well-paid career?

Tom Hopkins
    Professional sales trainer, speaker, and author of *How to Master the Art of Selling* (<u>www.tomhopkins.com</u>)

The highest price paid for
any form of ability in the world is
a master salesperson with a
creative imagination.

Chapter One

Nothing Happens Until Somebody Sells Something

*This is the basis of what moves the
entire free enterprise system!*

Mary Kay Ash created a cosmetics empire in direct sales and used that platform to empower hundreds of thousands of women to succeed. Though she passed away in 2001, her life, teachings, and example continue to inspire and encourage people around the world. The business world will forever feel her impact.

She could sell!

As a mother with three children to support, **Mary Kay** juggled selling on a part-time basis while taking pre-med courses at a local college. Then one day she took an aptitude test that changed everything. The results were in: her selling ability outranked her science ability!

Being one to take action, she quit school and chose to sell for Stanley Home Products, a direct sales company. She knew what she wanted and needed to accomplish. She wrote her weekly sales goals in soap on her bathroom mirror, then she took action, scheduling three

> Bill Gates is smart, but he became the richest man in the world because of his creative imagination and selling skills.

home-demonstration appointments every single day. As a result, she won one sales competition after another.

Hungry for more, she went to work for another company, and set more sales records, becoming their national training director. It was then that she hit the glass ceiling. A male colleague she had trained was promoted ahead of her, and at twice her salary. It was wrong, and she knew it!

So **she took action.** After 25 years in direct sales, setting records on every front, she called it quits. She retired.

Sales and related occupations are expected to increase nearly 10% to 16.8 million jobs by 2014.

But **she couldn't sit still.** Her retirement lasted for an entire month and then she was back to work. "To me, work and growth were the same thing," she said.

Work, this time around, meant doing something where she was in control. She could sell and she knew she wanted to help other women. With that heart, she began to write a how-to career book for women. The book just so happened to be a marketing plan for a "dream company."

"Before long," **Mary Kay** said, "I began asking myself, 'Why are you theorizing about a dream company? Why don't you just start one?'" Wanting to be in business for herself, she bought the formula for a skin care cream that she had been using and enlisted her husband to handle operations. She **began recruiting friends** to be independent beauty consultants for her new venture, which she called "Beauty by Mary Kay."

At the time of her death in 2001, Mary Kay Inc. had over 800,000 representatives in more than 30 markets, an independent sales force of more than 1.7 million, and annual sales of more than $2.25 billion. She was a master at selling!

Sadly, one month before her company launched, her husband died suddenly. **Mary Kay** wanted to stop, but her two sons and daughter encouraged her to pursue her dreams. "I knew I would never have a second chance to put my dream into action," she later wrote. So on Friday, September 13, 1963, her own **"there-is-no-glass-ceiling"** company was formally in business.

Mary Kay Inc. ended the first year with a profit! Five years later the company went public (and then private again in 1985).

Avon Products, Amway, and Mary Kay combined have over 9 millions sales associates in the U.S. These companies are the top three in terms of largest sales forces for U.S. direct sales companies.

Today, her company remains one of the largest privately held firms in the United States. **Mary Kay** did all she could to benefit the women who joined her company, giving them financial opportunity, words of praise, and awards, including the famous pink Cadillac.

She was selling every step of the way!

With an incredible track record, Mary Kay Inc. has been considered one of the finest business opportunities for women. More than 400 women worldwide have average annual incomes well into six figures and more than 200 in the United States have earned commissions in excess of $1 million. **They did this by choosing selling as a career.**

When **Mary Kay Ash** died in 2001, there were over 800,000 sales representatives in Mary Kay Inc. Currently, the independent sales force numbers more than 1.7 million and the company's annual sales exceed $2.25 billion!

Starting as a brand assistant, Susan Arnold rose through the ranks to become the first woman to reach a president-level position in the $76 billion Proctor & Gamble company. She knows how to sell!

The Basis Of All Success

Selling is the basis of all success. **The truth is, nothing happens until someone sells something.** Houses are built, but if they are not sold, nobody gets paid, companies shut down, employees are laid off, people have fewer choices, prices increase, commissions are not paid, agencies get smaller, and taxes increase.

- Computers are made, **but if they are not sold ...**

- Cars are built, **but if they are not sold ...**

- Schools are opened, **but if students don't show up ...**

- Churches are built, **but if people don't come ...**

- Fields are planted, **but if the crops aren't sold ...**

The list is limitless, but the point is this: **THE WORLD REVOLVES AROUND SELLING**. Every area of life is intrinsically linked to someone who sold something to someone else. Or look at it this way.

What good is a rocket **without fuel?**

What good is a computer **without electricity?**

What good is a car **without wheels?**

What good is a cell phone **without batteries?**

What good is a supermarket **without produce?**

Multi-millionaire Henry Penix once purchased a three million dollar facility for one dollar, sold it within 90 days for $600,000, and used that cash to fund another multi-million-dollar deal that closed within the next 30 days. Only someone with a creative imagination and sales ability could pull that off!

What good is a movie theater **without a movie?**

What good is a sailboat **without a sail?**

It all comes down to selling, and selling is the basis of all success.

We Are All In Sales

There are only two reasons that we do anything: *to gain a benefit or to avoid a loss.* And to gain the benefit or avoid the loss, **we sell**.

From the moment we draw our first breath and cry for food until our last breath and we ask for comfort, we are selling. It doesn't matter what package we come in. *We are all in sales.*

Could a litigation attorney convince a jury on any point without persuasion, convincing, facts, presenting, speaking, etc? It's **all part of selling.**

Could a man courting a woman be doing anything but selling himself? His mannerism, body language, actions, words, clothes, and cologne are all part of selling himself to the woman in his life.

Parents talking to their children about values and principles are convincing them to take the same path. **That is selling!**

The facts are …

- a presentation to a bank is *selling*

- a promotion is the result of *selling*

- a lawyer is *selling* the jury

> The McDonald brothers made a good hamburger, but it was Ray Kroc who single-handedly turned McDonald's into a multi-billion dollar empire. How? Ray could sell!

- a person with an idea is *selling* it to prospective investors

- every leader is *selling* vision

- websites are *selling*

- doctors are *selling* treatments

- peer pressure is *selling*

- children are *selling*

Everyone is selling something … **and so are you!** You might not agree with that statement, but in attempting to prove me wrong, you are only proving me right.

You sell me your idea and I'll sell you mine. And since we all spend more time selling than any other activity besides sleeping, **it only makes sense that we become master salespeople.**

Become A Master Salesperson!

Let me ask you this: Who are the highest paid lawyers? Those who can sell the jury! Who are the highest paid doctors, athletes, actors, etc.? Those who can sell will always be the highest paid, regardless of the occupation!

Consider **Christopher Columbus**, credited with discovering the Americas on his famous voyage of 1492. He convinced the Spanish King and Queen to finance his voyage to discover a <u>non-existent passage</u> to the Far East! *He had been trying to sell the vision for a decade*, but history was made when he made the sale.

W. Clement Stone started with $100 and a creative imagination and built the largest exclusive accident insurance company in the United States. He was a master salesman!

Or what about **Ray Kroc**, the genius behind the McDonald's industry? Brothers **Dick** and **Mac McDonald** ran an effective hamburger restaurant. Ray told them about his idea of opening several of the same restaurants across the nation, but their response was, "Who could we get to open them for us?" Ray replied, "What about me?"

As business grew, **Ray** was always more convinced of the potential than the **McDonald** brothers, so he bought them out for a mere $2.7 million dollars. Doing business in over 110 nations today, *the multi-billion dollar business of McDonald's* would never have come to pass without Ray Kroc's **ability to sell**.

> According to the U.S. Department of Labor, 14,000,000 people are employed in sales positions. This includes everything: direct selling, network marketing, showroom automobile salespeople, manufacturers' representatives, all people in the financial sector, retail stores and shops, pharmaceutical sales, and much more.

The businesses and organizations that will change the world will be the ones who have master salespeople working for them. Similarly, the people who will affect your future and who have already changed your history are master salespeople.

Become a master salesperson yourself. I can promise you that you will be very glad you did!

I simply love selling! I am passionate about selling. I love to sell, and as far as I'm concerned, selling is the greatest profession on earth! There's no high in the world to match it!

Like a poet loves to write!

Cosmetics queen, Estée Lauder, never worked a day in her life without selling. She notes, "If I believe in something, I sell it, and I sell it hard." She was a master salesperson!

Like an artist loves to paint!

Like a singer loves to sing!

Like a marathoner loves to run!

Like a pilot loves to fly!

I get a "high" from selling! And I want to sell you on the incredible profession, career, and occupation of selling. I want to sell you on what you become as a result.

If you could be anything, be a salesperson!

If you want the attributes of the master salespeople and want to become what they have become ... *choose selling*.

If you want to have the income that master salespeople enjoy ... *choose selling.*

Most chief executive officers of the Fortune 700 companies have backgrounds that include sales and marketing.

If you have been downsized, "rightsized," terminated, or laid off ... *choose selling*.

If you are dissatisfied with your current income, not to mention your income potential ... *choose selling*.

If you are a female and you think you are limited, passed over, or that you've hit the glass ceiling ... *choose selling*.

If you are a college student trying to decide on a profession ... *choose selling*.

Ross Perot left IBM with creative ideas and salesmanship and built a company that made him a multi-billionaire.

If you have been discriminated against because of your accent, education, color, race, or the side of the tracks you grew up on … *choose selling*.

If you have been overlooked one too many times or been relegated to a place in the business that gives you no hope of a future within the company … *choose selling*.

If you are tired of being told what to do, when to do it, how to do it, where to do it, and why to do it and you want to be free to be your own person … *choose selling*.

If you dream of a bigger car, a nicer home, or even more children, but you can't see it happening on your current budget… *choose selling*.

For many, network marketing is the best way to take advantage of the selling opportunity. They begin on a part-time basis, then move to full-time when their sales income exceeds their job's income. Robert Kiyosaki, author of *Rich Dad, Poor Dad*, says, "Network marketing is open to anyone who has drive, determination, and perseverance. You don't need to be wealthy beforehand, and you don't need degrees from prestigious universities. The opportunity is there for anyone and everyone who seizes it."

If you feel like life is battleship gray and you long for the vibrant colors of a bright future … *choose selling*.

Salespeople are the ones who write their own paychecks. There are no limitations! They have independence. They control their own time. They carve out their own destiny. They are the ones that companies want to hire. They are the ones that companies want to promote. And they are often the ones who end up leading the company!

At age 30, A. L. Williams was a high school coach making $10,700 a year. Twenty years later, he was chairman of his own company, the world's largest producer of individual life insurance. During the 1980s, his company outsold Prudential and New York Life. His success came from his ability to sell himself and his ideas!

If you want to reach the top, and possibly be the CEO, president, or owner ... *choose selling.*

You cannot find any other profession that makes these claims!

As you can see, or maybe you already know, selling **is by far the greatest profession in the world!**

I've written this book to convince and persuade you to get into selling! You can do the greatest good on earth by being a master sales-person.

Nothing Happens Until Somebody Sells Something

Today, **Ross Perot** is a household name, but it didn't start that way. At age seven, **Ross** started selling, which over the years included such things as selling Christmas cards, breaking horses, selling magazines, selling garden seeds, buying and selling saddles, delivering newspapers, and collecting for classified ads.

One favored quality for CEOs: a marketing/sales career background.

After high school, he spent four years in the United States Navy. In 1957, **Ross** and his wife moved to Dallas and he went to work as a salesman for IBM's data processing division.

Bill Kloster, "Mr. Dr Pepper," never studied marketing, but he succeeded in selling because he knew how to sell from his heart. At age 14, he started working at the Dublin, Texas, bottling plant for a mere $0.10 an hour. His love for Dr. Pepper and his ability to sell and promote pushed him higher and higher, and in 1991, Bill-the-manager became Bill-the-owner of the Dublin Dr. Pepper plant and franchise. Throughout his life, the small Dr. Pepper franchise was continuously among the top 10 producers in per capita consumption. From bottle sorter to company owner ... all because of his ability to sell!

In 1962, with a $1,000 loan from his wife, Perot started Electronic Data Systems (EDS). Over the next 22 years, he built EDS into one of the world's largest technology services firms. He is a master salesperson!

In 1984, **Ross** sold EDS to General Motors for $2.5 billion, *but he was not done selling*. In 1988, he founded a new technology services company, Perot Systems Corporation. He served as Chief Executive Officer until 1992 and again from 1997 until 2000, helping to take the company public in 1999. Perot served as Chairman of the Board until 2004, when he was elected Chairman Emeritus.

Ross Perot learned a long time ago that **nothing happens until you sell something**.

Irene Rosenfeld, Chairman and CEO of Kraft Foods, started her career with General Foods as an associate market research manager. She knows what sells!

Nothing Happens Until
Somebody Sells Something

Chapter One:
Summary

1. **Selling is the basis of all success; the world revolves around selling.** Every area of life is intrinsically linked to someone who sold something to someone else.

2. **There are only two reasons we do anything: to gain a benefit or to avoid a loss.** To gain the benefit or avoid the loss, we sell. We are all in sales.

3. **Become a master salesperson.** Those who can sell will always be the highest paid, regardless of the occupation. The businesses and organizations that will change the world will be the ones who have master salespeople working for them.

4. **Selling is by far the greatest profession in the world.** You can do the greatest good on earth by being a master salesperson.

5. **Nothing happens until somebody sells something.**

I wake up every morning without giving any mental recognition to the possibility of defeat.
If they sit, I sell.

Chapter Two

What Salespeople Have

And the rest of the world wants, too!

Bill Gates is known for being thc **richest man** in the world. **Gates** has been likened to **Henry Ford**, who struck it big in the business world with a design that brought new technology to the masses and revolutionized America in the process.

Gates first became interested in computers when, at age six, he attended the 1962 World Fair. Later, in middle school, a computer company offered his friends and him the opportunity to work on one of their systems in exchange for free computer time.

In a short time, they had finished their contracted work and were no longer allowed the free computer time. The young men hacked their way back into the computer system, much to the surprise of the company.

Nina Tassler is a risk taker. And she can sell! This is how she became CBS Entertainment President, breaking barriers as a woman and a Latina. She latches onto risky projects and can sell them. Sure enough, they become hits, but Nina already knew that. She knows what sells and how to sell it.

During their high school years, **Gates** and his friends did everything they could to gain more computer experience, and as a result, were hired to write payroll and scheduling programs.

For a couple of years, **Gates** studied computer science at Harvard. He dropped out and was hired by a computer manufacturer in Arizona to write the software for their computers, modifying the old standard BASIC coding. As a result of that first poorly written royalties agreement, Microsoft's approach to selling its products was drastically changed. **Gates** decided that licensing their software programs would be better than selling it outright to IBM, leaving Microsoft open to sell their operating system (DOS) to other computer makers.

A brilliant move for a master salesperson with a creative imagination!

Within a few short years, DOS became the standard operating system of nearly every computer. Microsoft was at the forefront of the software industry with the development of their applications software — especially spreadsheets and word processing. In 1985 Microsoft released the Windows operating system, now the standard in all personal computers.

Another incredible idea that every salesperson can admire!

Microsoft's aggressive marketing strategies combined with **Gates'** vision for the computer industry have led to enormous profits and is the envy of virtually every business.

Obviously, Bill Gates is an incredible salesperson!

In 2005, Brenda Barnes became Chairman and CEO of Sara Lee, after a long string of sales and marketing positions. Who better qualified to run a company than a master salesperson!

What Top Salespeople Have

What are master salespeople like? What qualities do they possess that set them apart from the rest? Here is something interesting to consider: **Everyone who accomplishes anything in life possesses the same attributes as master salespeople.**

In fact, to accomplish your goals and dreams and to become the person you want to be and are capable of becoming, you will need these same attributes.

The question is: **what is it that master salespeople have?**

After more than six decades of sales experience, whether it was leading the sales force through personal production or leading the sales force because I owned the company, I've found that all top salespeople, all top performers, all successful people ... have these five distinct attributes:

ATTRIBUTE #1 — they live with positive expectancy

Top salespeople have a positive attitude and operate with positive expectancy. They are upbeat, they see the cup as half full, and they are always expecting a positive result from any day's effort.

Simply put, they are eternal optimists. Consequently, they not only believe that they will make the sale, they also believe that the people they talk to:

- **want to buy,**
- **want to keep buying,**
- **want to be their clients,**
- **want to give referrals, and**
- **want to be their friend.**

Christopher Columbus sold his dream voyage
for 10 years before he actually set sail!

Their positive mindset carries them over every roadblock they encounter. After all, roadblocks are merely stepping-stones on the way to success!

We all know the psychological truth that a single mind cannot be divided against itself. It's impossible, no matter how hard you try, to think of failure in one direction and success in the other.

The Bureau of Labor Statistics estimates that between 2000 and 2014, total employment in the U.S. will increase to 164.5 million employees. Of that figure, it is anticipated that approximately 16.8 million will be employed in sales and related occupations.

That being the case, your mind is either dominated by success and positive thoughts or it is dominated by failure and negative thoughts. As a result, *you always end up with what has been preoccupying your mind.*

The top salespeople who have a positive attitude have more prospects and customers than they can handle. There is nothing mystical about it … *that's just the way it is!*

In fact, top salespeople have such a positive attitude that *they believe everyone is out to do only good to them!* That positive attitude shines through in every other area of life, and the results speak for themselves.

ATTRIBUTE #2 — contagious enthusiasm

Enthusiasm **paves the way for you and your ideas**. It makes people more receptive to what you are saying. It affects our body chemistry and their body chemistry as well.

Bill Armor became wealthy and rubbed shoulders with the elitist of the elite because he possessed one thing: enthusiasm. I have been his close friend for years, and I can say without the slightest exaggeration that Bill had more enthusiasm than an entire football team! He is a master of the art of selling.

When I sold life insurance, I believed in my product so much that I never met another person who had more life insurance than I did. In my presentation, if my prospects said they already had a life insurance policy worth a certain amount, I would reply, **"That's nothing, look at this!"**

Then I would take my insurance policies that I had connected together and flip them open like cascading stairs. My prospective clients were always impressed, simply because I believed 100% in my product. The truth about enthusiasm is that once you learn the product or service you are selling, 85% of your sales come as the result of your own enthusiasm.

Enthusiasm sells. It shows that you believe in your product or service. Such a belief is not only necessary, *it is contagious as well!* Your excitement flows out of everything you say and do. It affects how you see people, how you serve them, and how they respond to you.

Passionate enthusiasm attracts people, overcomes objections, and is virtually impenetrable to distractions.

This is why top salespeople not only have enthusiasm that is *contagious*, but they have enthusiasm that is *maintained*.

ATTRIBUTE #3 — passionate desire

The top producers have a fire in their belly. **They have a passionate desire to excel.** They are motivated to take whatever action is necessary to reach their goals. And they do not know the meaning of "quit."

Desire **is not** a dark secret available to only a select few. Anyone, including you, can develop the desire that will make you a winner and that will bring you whatever it is you want.

> Larry Smith was fired from corporate America. "Too old" to start over, Larry chose selling. Today he enjoys a multiple six-figure income and is able to positively influence the lives of hundreds of people. And one added perk: he will never be fired again!

But the amount of desire you develop depends on you alone; others cannot do it for you. You can succeed only if you want success badly enough. Others may give you some help and moral support, but YOU must provide the desire and the self-motivation.

AutoNation's more than 250 car dealerships generate nearly $19 billion in U.S. sales annually, with approximately 4,000 salespeople. America's companies need more good salespeople.

When I first decided that I wanted a career as a professional salesman, I wanted to succeed so strongly that I was willing to give whatever effort and dedication was required to achieve my goal. The first nine months of my sales career was a financial disaster. I knew nothing about the techniques of selling and I met resistance on every hand.

For example, I was fired from one selling job by a sales manager who told me I didn't have what it took to succeed in the industry. He also told me that I was too quiet.

And on top of that, an older man who was a friend of our family advised me to quit selling. He said my father had intended for me to be a cabinet-maker, a plumber, or an electrician, and that the people in all those trades were making a lot of money.

Although I loved and respected him, he could not arouse in me any desire to quit. My desire was already focused on winning in the game of selling. I moved forward and never looked back ... **and won in a very big way! I mean a very, very BIG way!**

Top salespeople know that desire is the dynamic motivation behind every worthwhile purpose; it is the inspiration that keeps the flames of progress

In 1987, three seasoned restaurant employees (Tim Gannon, Bob Basham, and Chris Sullivan) decided to launch out on their own. They knew the industry, they persevered, and they could sell. Combined, these ingredients made Outback Steakhouse a smashing success.

burning. That is because in the long run we become what we purpose and we gain for ourselves what we really desire.

ATTRIBUTE #4 — *self-confidence*

Top salespeople have a self-confidence that is second to none! And naturally following right behind their indomitable self-confidence is a very good self-image.

Why do top salespeople possess such self-confidence? The answer: because they know how to *produce* self-confidence.

Top salespeople know that genuine confidence comes only from know-how, know-how comes only from experience, and experience comes only from doing, getting involved, and taking action.

In short, action produces confidence. So many people, salespeople included, lack the confidence they need to be successful, yet they aren't willing to do what it takes to gain the confidence they desperately need.

Many years ago, a soft-spoken, shy 5'4" tall man joined one of our sales teams. I periodically checked on his progress. This individual, after making 50 presentations in two months, hadn't made a single sale!

Several months later, he was up to 150 presentations and still without a sale. I was beginning to question his desire to be a salesman. "I'm getting better," he kept saying.

How did Ann Moore reach the top and become the Chairman and CEO of Time, Inc., the biggest gorilla in the US magazine business with 126 titles and nearly one-fifth of the industry's ad spending? She started in corporate finance, and, as you would expect, also held numerous consumer marketing positions. Master salespeople simply rise to the top!

Finally, after the 200th presentation, the sales began to come. **The sales *had* to start coming!** By taking a LOT of action, his experience and know-how increased to the point that he began to make sales.

What happened to this "loser" of a salesman? **His sales increased until he was making over a million dollars a year in commissions before he retired!**

And this top salesman's level of self-confidence? As you would expect, it was through the roof! You would have thought he was 12' tall, rather than his mere 5'4".

Top salespeople have a no-limitations belief in themselves. They know where they are, where they are going, and how to get there. They are goal directed. And they are not easily distracted or knocked off track.

The truth is, nobody can stop you when you are self-confident, but without self-confidence, success is unlikely. That is because, as all top salespeople know, *self-confidence is power!*

ATTRIBUTE #5 — persistence

Top salespeople have an I-will-not-be-denied attitude. As a result, they hang on until they reach their goals. They have learned not to let rejection, anyone's opinions, or previous failures weigh them down. They press on, regardless.

Persistence is what **Thomas Edison** called "stick-to-itiveness." His legendary 10,000 failed attempts at making a light bulb rank him as one of the most persistent people of all time!

Linda Vance was part of a direct sales company that opened for business in a foreign country. She didn't know a soul in that country, but she jumped on a plane anyway. Within five days, she was in business. Linda can sell!

In the early 1960s, while working to grow my first company, I made the commitment to write my first personal development program.

My commitment was: "If I am alive, every Tuesday and Thursday from 9 p.m. to midnight, I will work on this course."

I built my whole work schedule around that commitment. It took me six years from start to finish for that program. When I took it to several publishers, they were not interested, so I printed it myself, **sold it myself, and recruited other people to sell it**.

One of Paul J. Meyer's many different programs boasts sales of over $700 million, making it the top selling personal development program in history. His commissions and royalties were over $100 million from that one program!

Since it was introduced, sales of that one program are now …

over $700 million!

That is more than any other personal development program or course in history. **My commissions and royalties were over $100 million alone from that one program!**

Combining persistency with an I-will-not-be-denied attitude puts you in the top percentages of anyone in any category!

Nobody is born with these attributes. **They are learned … *and they are chosen*.** You must choose to have these five attributes.

Make them yours. **You can if you choose.**

When you want them bad enough, you will have them. That is certain.

Best-selling author, Ken Blanchard, can write, speak, and teach. He is an incredible communicator, trainer, and businessman. But I know him and I'll guarantee you that his greatest skill by far is his ability to sell!

What Salespeople Have

Two childhood friends, **Rich** and **Jay**, had a dream to own their own business. In high school, Jay drove a 1931 Model A Ford and Rich would pay $0.25 a week for rides to school. Along the way, they would dream and plan together.

After World War II, they launched a flight school and a drive-in restaurant. They sold out in 1948. Soon after, they were introduced to a food supplement company that sold products via direct selling.

Their entrepreneurial lights burned with a whole new intensity.

They saw this as opportunity for the average person to own a business!

Their success as sales reps convinced them that anyone who was willing to work hard could have a successful business of their own if they used the direct selling approach.

Eager to try it themselves, they formed the Ja-Ri Corporation and sold vitamins and food supplements. The Ja-Ri company offered a low risk business opportunity and had no territorial or income limits, but it offered unlimited potential for anyone willing to work hard.

Rich and **Jay** had found what they were looking for! Hard work combined with a good business model equaled success. **It was, they reasoned, the American way. From this came a new name for this business: Amway.**

Sheryl Sandberg successfully spearheaded many advertising products for the highly successful Internet company, Google. Her division accounts for more than 50% of the company's billions in revenue. As VP of Global Online Sales and Operations, she is making waves because of her creative imagination and her ability to sell!

The first Amway product was a biodegradable household cleaner and they sold it from their basements. The next year, they moved to an abandoned service station. The business grew and its distributors sold soap, shaving cream, furniture polish, detergent, cookware, cosmetics, and other goods.

The company motto was: **"You can do it, too."**

The idea that someone with no sales experience could make a lot of money on a part-time or full-time basis selling household items was revolutionary!

Sales for the first year reached an impressive $500,000, but **Rich** and **Jay** wanted to take the opportunity to the world!

In the 1960s, they expanded to Canada, Asia, Europe, and Australia. By that time, they had a network of more than 100,000 distributors, more than $85 million in sales, 200 products being manufactured at Amway's complex in Ada, Michigan, and more than 700 employees.

By the end of the 1970s, sales were nearly $800 million, and Amway's sales passed the billion-dollar mark in the 1980s.

Now known as Quixtar in the US and Canada, Amway has since grown to 13,000 employees and has more than 3 million distributors in more than 80 countries and territories around the world. Worldwide sales are over $6 billion, with China being its largest market.

Ettore Boiardi was a chef who could sell. He opened his own restaurant, Il Giardino d'Italia, at age 28, and patrons asked for his spaghetti sauce so often that he had to use a factory to keep up with demand. He then went national with his products. At the time of his death in 1985, Chef Boyardee products were bringing in $500 million per year. This chef could sell!

Two boys dreamed big dreams, and then took action to make those dreams become a reality.

In their many years of business together, **Rich DeVos** and **Jay Van Andel** built their business into a multi-billion dollar international corporation and one of the world's largest direct selling companies. **They are masters of the game of selling. Their motivation to change people's lives and to give them a better future helped fuel their success.**

Only through selling could you accomplish such a feat! And what is incredible is this: the same opportunity that **Rich** and **Jay** discovered back in 1948 ... is wide open to you today if you choose!

Mark Seguin grew up in a gypsy lifestyle. He had no education, didn't learn to read until age 14, and only knew how to shoe horses. Today, Mark earns a multiple six-figure income because he chose selling.

What Salespeople Have

Chapter Two:
Summary

1. **Everyone who accomplishes anything in life possesses the same attributes as master salespeople.** All top salespeople have these five distinct attributes: positive expectancy, contagious enthusiasm, passionate desire, self-confidence, and persistence.

2. **Top salespeople live with positive expectancy; they are eternal optimists.** This positive mindset carries them over every roadblock.

3. **They have contagious enthusiasm and enthusiasm sells.** Once you learn the product or service you are selling, 85% of your sales come as a result of your own enthusiasm.

4. **The top producers have a fire in their belly – a passionate desire to excel.** You can succeed only if you want success badly enough. You must provide the desire and the self-motivation.

5. **Top salespeople have strong self-confidence and a very good self-image.** They have a no-limitations belief in themselves.

6. **They are persistent and hang on until they reach their goals.** Importantly, they have learned not to let rejections, anyone's opinions, or previous failures weigh them down.

7. **These five attributes – positive expectancy, contagious enthusiasm, passionate desire, self-confidence, and persistence – are learned and chosen.** You must choose to have them.

I believe that every client, every prospect, and every person alive benefits by getting to know me and buying what I have to offer. Success is imminent.

Chapter Three

What Salespeople Can Become

And the rest of the world is jealous!

Donald J. Trump is known the world over for money, work, and interests in real estate, gaming, sports, and entertainment. He is a deal-maker without peer. **But there is no doubt, his greatest ability is his ability to sell. If he is talking, he is selling.**

Trump started young in his father's New York real estate business, and by the 1970s had made quite a name for himself in the Manhattan area, somehow selling the banks and city government on financing his ambitious developments! He built the grandiose Trump Tower on Fifth Avenue in 1982 and soon moved into the casino business in New Jersey.

Trump went on the skids in 1990, finding himself over $900 million in debt and facing bankruptcy. **But ever the dealmaker, persuader, convincer, and salesman**, he rebounded and by 2000 he was again worth over a billion dollars. **Trump** currently owns over 18 million square feet of prime Manhattan real estate.

> Lee Iacocca did the impossible! He sold the government on financing Chrysler (to the tune of $1.5 billion) and he sold the American people on buying his cars. Within three years, Chrysler was back on its feet and the loan was repaid!

And, in a departure from his real estate acquisitions, **Trump** and NBC are partners in the ownership and broadcast rights for the three largest beauty competitions in the world: the Miss Universe, Miss USA, and Miss Teen USA Pageants.

His books and TV show have increased his image and popularity. You don't have to agree or disagree with **Donald Trump** to accept the fact **that he can sell**!

He could have never become the larger-than-life person that he is today if it were not for his **ability to sell**. He could not have come back from the edge of bankruptcy if it were not for his **ability to sell**.

When you become a master salesperson, you add 2 + 2 and get 6! There is certain multiplication that takes place deep within you when you sell. Every master salesperson knows exactly what I'm talking about.

The top 20 automotive-dealer organizations generate more than $77.2 billion in total revenues, with a sales force of just under 20,000. The average annual sales per salesperson is $3.8 million for these mega-dealers.

What Top Salespeople Become

What is it that master salespeople become? **After more than six decades of selling and five decades of creating personal development programs that have changed millions of lives**, I have found that:

- **all top salespeople ...**
- **all top performers ...**
- **all successful people ...**

have become something they were not when they first started.

Anita Roddick, who founded The Body Shop chain of beauty product stores, feels that selling is creating a product or service so good that people will pay for it. She knows how to sell herself and her products!

They have become something that is more than they originally were. They have multiplied, stretched, and grown. In every case, what they become includes these five qualities:

QUALITY #1 — persuasive and convincing

Top salespeople **are the best persuaders and convincers**. They use stories, dreams, and color. They paint the pictures, whether literally or imaginary, for people to see.

For me, it's a habit. It's intentional. When I'm talking with people, I make sure they can see it like I can. Usually, when they see things as I see them, the selling is done.

A few years ago I was in a meeting with about 30 other people. We were there to discuss a fundraising project for the Boys and Girls Clubs in our city. We were told that the most money raised in this small town was $1 million, but our goal was $2 million to be pledged over three years.

When it came my turn to speak, because I love kids and am sold on what the Boys and Girls Clubs is doing, I was very passionate and painted a clear picture of what we all could do. **When lunch was over, we had pledges for over $750,000! And from there we went on to sell the dream and exceeded our $2 million goal.**

The power to persuade has even been called **"the most important skill a leader can develop."** This is absolutely true, but you don't have to be completely straight-faced and serious about it. Humor can be a part.

Wayne Huizenga of Waste Management Inc. and Block-busters understands that he has to get to know people face-to-face and develop a sincere relationship. That way, if they run into problems in a deal, it doesn't get adversarial. "We trust each other and have the confidence we can work things out."

Just recently, I wanted to get a loan from a certain bank. The loan was in process but it was taking weeks, and could take several more weeks to complete. I sent an email to the bank owner that said, "Please laugh when you read this, but getting a loan from your bank is like trying to herd turtles through peanut butter."

He replied that day, "I personally made sure that your loan was pushed through the peanut butter … you have your loan!"

Nobody knows the full power of persuasion and convincing and story telling, but top salespeople come the closest to experiencing it … *and they are also the ones who benefit from it the most!*

QUALITY #2 — focused on service

All top professional salespeople have a keen focus on service. They believe and act upon the Golden Rule of service: *serve others as you would like to be served.*

What is the result? People want to be their clients. They want to buy. They are comfortable buying from someone they trust. They want to give referrals. They want to do all they can to help you succeed.

In effect, through a focus on service, top salespeople are creating for themselves small centers of influence. Over time, this creates a ground swell of momentum, support, and sales … a position that every sales-person dreams of being in!

For example, not long ago I was at the Thai Orchid restaurant in the Cayman Islands. From the moment I walked in, I experienced the best service in a restaurant that I can remember. It was incredible, and the food was equally as amazing!

> Master salesman Chad Henley lost his job when the phar-maceutical company he worked for decided to reduce its sales force. Within weeks, Chad had multiple job offers, but was rehired by the same company. Master sales-people are always in hot demand.

Within a week I had already told more than a dozen people about the restaurant. I will do all I can to recommend them, promote them, and bring them business. In effect, I have become a center of influence for them, *simply because they focused on service!*

The power to persuade has even been called, "The most important skill a leader can develop."

Salespeople who focus on service are also the same ones who have a long-term outlook that anticipates building the business over a period of time.

They are serious about their business because they are serious about taking care of you.

The reverse is also true: customers, clients, and prospects know immediately by your service if you are serious about your business. **Without service, you have little chance of getting repeat business.**

To understate one of the most powerful forces that the top salespeople enjoy: *service speaks volumes!*

QUALITY #3 — full of integrity in all things

Top salespeople are **honest, keep their word, work hard, take responsibility, are dependable, don't blame others**, and **act conscientiously**.

In short, they operate with integrity. They have to, because with integrity, their business grows, but without integrity, their business shrivels up. It is inevitable.

Dana Walden is Chairman of 20th Century Fox Television. She started as a publicist for such Fox shows as "The X-Files," but she rose to become the president in less than 10 years. How? She knew what sold and how to sell it!

Many years ago I was selling juice dispensers with plans to get a franchise of my own. But after a month of selling, I discovered some information about the company that undermined my confidence in the product and the franchising possibilities. When I discussed my findings with the owner, he dismissed me as being young, inexperienced, immature, and flat out wrong.

Being able to motivate yourself to accomplish your own goals is one of the most powerful assets anyone could possess.

Instead of doing nothing, I immediately called the individuals I had sold on the product and its franchising potential and recommended that they get a refund since it was still within the three-month trial period. When my boss found out, he was livid and fired me on the spot, but I was on my way out the door anyway.

How could I continue to sell something I didn't believe in? And since I saw holes in the business plan, how could I willingly let other people who trusted me run the risk of losing their money? I couldn't do either of these, so I left the company.

What happened to my clients? Today, decades later, if I were to present them with a product, service, or business opportunity, **they would still be receptive!** Why? Because I operated with integrity to their benefit … and people NEVER forget that.

Top salesman with one of America's leading pharmaceutical companies, Tim Smith, says it best: "**Trust is essential to successful selling because customers don't buy from people they can't trust**."

Tim, like every top salesperson, understands that the bond of trust develops when you operate with integrity.

Only someone with incredible selling skills could be President and CEO of the world's #1 e-commerce brand, Ebay! And that master salesperson is Meg Whitman.

I've always communicated, whether with words or actions, that I back up what I say. Anyone who does business with me or my family has a guarantee that they will never be treated unfairly. We are sales people. We see the big picture and the value of every customer of our product and service, for the long haul.

QUALITY #4 — self-motivating

Top salespeople are **self-motivators**. They motivate themselves **to take action regardless of how they feel, regardless of the circumstances around them**, and **regardless of what others say, think, or do**.

The phrase, **"The highest price paid for any form of ability in the world is a master salesperson with a creative imagination,"** aptly describes self-motivated salespeople.

Being able to motivate yourself to accomplish your own goals is one of the most powerful assets anyone could possess. Unfortunately, self-motivation is seldom utilized. Instead, sales organizations and sales managers regularly resort to temporary motivation tactics.

Don't get me wrong, I'm not saying that temporary tactics don't work. **They do work, but they are only temporary.** As soon as an incentive loses its power to excite you or a fear ceases to alarm you, the power it had to motivate you is gone. Don't talk about fear or incentive motivation. Talk only about self-motivation.

Self-motivation is the **only long-term form of motivation**. Every top salesperson is internally motivated to excel, to succeed, and to win. Sure, it requires the development of inner strength, conscious willpower, overwhelming desire, and the determination to reach any

---

Oprah Winfrey, one of the wealthiest women in North America, has learned to be in the right place at the right time. Some call it luck, but it's nothing less than selling. Oprah Winfrey is a master saleswoman!

---

goal you personally want to achieve, *but only those who are self-motivated will win in the end.*

Self-motivated individuals are the ones who dream big dreams **AND** take the necessary little steps on a daily basis to get there. They are the ones who make **affirmations** like these a natural part of their thinking:

- **I am a great salesperson.**

- **I've earned the right, more than anyone, to make this presentation.**

- **I'll make the sale and I'll make a friend.**

- **I do not give mental recognition to the possibility of defeat.**

- **I'll do it now!**

Self-motivated salespeople are leaders. **They are the ones who win the race.** And they are the ones who have the highest incomes.

QUALITY #5 — full of love for people

The crème de la crème, the best of the best simply love people. Their love is displayed by the attitude of genuinely wanting you to be better off after they sell you something. They really, truly want you to benefit.

Frances Avrett was a greenhouse owner and mother of five when her husband was struck with a debilitating heart condition. Out of sheer need for more income, she chose selling ... and she is glad she did! She enjoyed great financial success and 18 more years with her husband before he died. His last words were, "I'm so proud of you." Frances needed to stay in charge, chose to stay in charge, and is a wealthy salesperson today!

Many years ago, I was interested in a piece of property. I stopped by the apartment complex, spoke to a friend of the owner, and put a down payment on the property. When I returned a couple days later to sign the papers, the man looked discouraged. He wasn't saying much, but I could tell something was bothering him.

Instead of moving ahead with the deal, I stopped and asked him what was wrong. He replied, "It's not your responsibility, but the owner of this property had promised me a certain percentage for selling it for him. Now that he has a committed buyer, he's backing out on the deal. That commission was going to be my retirement nest egg."

I immediately called the owner and said that the deal was off unless he would pay the promised amount to this man. Reluctantly, the owner agreed.

My new friend got his much-needed commission and I got the land I wanted. He knew I cared more about him than I did about making the deal. **This you-are-more-important-than-the-deal attitude spells out L-O-V-E in selling**, and top salespeople understand that. They genuinely care, from the little things to the big things, about their prospects and clients, and seek to do all they can to be of service.

As a result, top salespeople have more business than they can handle!

People who want to reach their goals and their dreams will possess these five qualities. **In fact, these attributes are the ONLY way they will reach their goals and dreams.**

The goal then as you move toward being a master salesperson is to make these qualities a part of your life, if they are not already, as

---

Former President, Ronald Reagan, could sell like few others. He sold the entire nation of America on regaining her position in the world. He could paint pictures with words and then sell you on doing just what he said. He was a master of the art of selling!

---

quickly as possible! It will take some work, but the benefits will make it entirely worth your while!

And when you choose to become a master salesperson, you will gain these qualities naturally, one step at a time, over a period of time.

What Salespeople Become

When **Ron Legrand** first got involved with real estate, he was a dead broke auto mechanic trying to make enough money to make ends meet. He was 35 years old, bankrupt, and he knew he didn't want to spend his future fixing cars in the hot Florida sun.

Every technological advance brings with it even greater opportunities to sell.

He wanted to sell. So, in the early 1980s, he attended a free seminar on how to buy real estate with no money or credit. From there, he borrowed $450 from friends (using his sales ability) to attend a two-day seminar.

He says, "That decision changed my life forever, my family's life, and their family's lives for generations to come."

Most of the information in the seminar was over his head, but he picked up one idea he felt he could do and within three weeks he made his first $3,000 from real estate using none of his own money or credit. *Again, he used his sales ability.*

Two years later his selling skills had helped him amass 276 units, some single family and some apartments units, not including those he sold along

Shelly Lazarus can sell! In the early 1990's, she won the American Express account for Ogilvy & Mather (the international advertising, marketing, and public relations agency that was founded in 1948) and made Ogilvy the exclusive agency for IBM. She hit it big, to say the least, and is now the Chairman and CEO of Ogilvy Worldwide.

the way for income. He was a millionaire ... on paper. He had over $1 million in equity two years after starting with no money or credit.

Each year his real estate empire grew and he learned more and more. Then he started teaching others to do what he had done. *Again, he was selling!*

Today, a multi-millionaire, he continues to teach and train others how to be successful in the real estate market. **Ron Legrand** is an example of someone with a **creative imagination, combined with a stellar sales ability, making it to the top!**

Master salespeople make more than any other profession. It's all about what you become as a master salesperson.

Andrea Jung, promoted to the position of Chairman and CEO of Avon Products in 1999, had the daunting task of trying to turn around a consumer products company that had a direct- selling business model that many felt was out of touch with modern business practices. It was a challenge, but nothing that master saleswoman Andrea Jung couldn't handle!

What Salespeople Can Become

Chapter Three:
Summary

1. **Top salespeople are the best persuaders and convincers.** They use stories, dreams, and color to paint the pictures, whether literally or imaginary, for people to see it like they can.

2. **They have a keen focus on service.** They believe and act upon the Golden Rule of Service: serve others as you would like to be served. The result is that people want to be their clients; customers are comfortable buying from someone they trust.

3. **They are full of integrity in all things.** Top salespeople are honest, keep their word, work hard, take responsibility, are dependable, don't blame others, and act conscientiously.

4. **Self-motivation is a quality top salespeople have.** They motivate themselves to take action regardless of how they feel, regardless of the circumstances around them, and regardless of what others say, think, or do.

5. **Top salespeople are full of love for people.** They genuinely want their customers to be better off after they sell them something. This you-are-more-important-than-the-deal attitude spells out L-O-V-E in selling.

6. **When you choose to become a master salesperson, you will gain these five qualities**: being persuasive and convincing; focused on service, full of integrity in all things, self-motivating; and full of love for people. These qualities are developed one step at a time, over a period of time.

Companies will bend over backwards to get a top salesperson on the team. They know the right salespeople can make all the difference!

Chapter Four

What Is Needed Most

*Every company and every country
needs great salespeople!*

Phil Knight is the man who turned an unknown company called Blue Ribbon Sports into Nike Corp., a multibillion-dollar enterprise and a household name. He has also made more money from athletics than anyone, ever. With a net worth of more than $7 billion, **Knight** ranks high up on Forbes's list of the richest Americans.

He did it by selling!

Blue Ribbon Sports cleared $3,240 in its first year, 1964. In fiscal year 2006, Nike's revenue surpassed $15 billion. "In a very short period of time, **Phil Knight** created one of the greatest American commerce stories of the 20th century," says sports agent David Falk, who has frequently butted heads with **Knight** over the marketing and representation of athletes.

If one of those athletes were not **Michael Jordan**, consumers worldwide might still be pronouncing "Nike" like "Mike." In large part

Deirdre Connelly rose through the ranks the old fashioned way ... she sold! Today, President of Lilly USA, a pharmaceutical company with more than 125 years of service, Deirdre continues to make an impact with her ability to sell.

because of that one person with a thousand-watt smile and spring-board legs, there is probably no greater status symbol among youths than Nike products.

Knight sold **Michael Jordan** on endorsing Nike shoes. That was a good sale!

Nike is what it is today because **Knight** understood and captured one of America's pop culture icons and married it to sports. Nike's marketing focused squarely on a charismatic athlete or image, rarely even mentioning or showing the shoes. The Nike swoosh is so ubiquitous that the name "Nike" is often omitted altogether.

According to the National Association of Sales Professionals (NASP), 10% of individuals employed in the U.S. are in sales-related positions.

How did he do it? Selling, selling, selling … with a creative imagination.

"**Phil** understands the symbolic power and attractiveness of sports," says A. Michael Spence, dean of the Stanford Graduate School of Business and a Nike board member. "And he helped build that connection in our culture."

Nike engineered shoes for top athletes to compete and train in. At the same time, the company's mass marketing sales model made the shoes so attractive and desirable that they became a required accessory to the American wardrobe and dream — even if teens only wore them to watch TV.

After returning from Japan in 1964, the 26-year-old **Knight** began selling Onitsuka running shoes from the back of his green Plymouth Valiant at

John Gardner, an attorney, had an excellent law practice but felt limited in his income possibilities. He chose selling and now has a multiple six-figure dollar income.

track meets across the Pacific Northwest. He was convinced that his inexpensive, high-performance shoes could beat the top "sneakers" — Adidas, Converse All-Stars, and Keds — in the market. By 1969, at the fortuitous dawn of the jogging boom, **Knight** sold a million dollars worth of Onitsuka shoes bearing his Blue Ribbon Sports label.

But he wanted more.

In 1971 it was time to give his fledgling company a new name and logo. **Knight** favored "Dimension Six," but his 45 employees thankfully laughed that one down. One employee proposed a name that came to him in a dream: Nike, for the Greek winged goddess of victory. The company paid $35 to commission a new logo, which resembled a fat checkmark and was dubbed a "swoosh." The new shoe debuted at the 1971 Olympic trials in Eugene, Oregon.

Nike sold $3.2 million worth of shoes in 1972 and its profits doubled each of the next 10 years. Nike passed Adidas to become the industry leader in the United States in 1980, the same year it went public.

How did **Knight** do it? **Selling, selling, selling … with a creative imagination.**

Today, the marketing continues, as such well-known athletes as **Tiger Woods** and **LeBron James** are signed with Nike.

What Is Needed Most

Every company in every country needs more creative sales people. Every charity, profession, and business needs more salespeople. Good salespeople. Why?

Verna Heath taught cheerleading until a disgruntled mother hired a hit man to kill her. Unwanted publicity, a divorce, and a movie deal that left her with nothing forced her to take action. She chose selling and built a sales team that extends across North America. She enjoys a life of freedom that could have only come through the profession of selling.

Because there is always room for more growth, more sales, and more work. **There simply can never be enough salespeople.**

On the other hand, people will argue that …

- **We have enough lawyers!**

- **We have enough taxi drivers!**

- **We have enough mechanics!**

- **We have enough plumbers!**

- **We have enough builders!**

- **We have enough politicians!**

I mean no disrespect to anyone who might have a profession that I've listed above, but I'm trying to make one thing crystal clear: *there is ALWAYS room for more professional salespeople*. Always!

There has never been a greater time to be a salesperson than today!

And that is a very good thing. No matter where you go, this need persists. In fact, the need is growing exponentially.

There has never been a greater time to be a salesperson than today! The opportunities are endless, and with the technological advances, you can

Bernard Rapoport started with nothing. He chose a business where he could use and develop his sales skills. He went on to build the largest insurance company, selling exclusively to union members. He sold it for tens of millions and continues to give away millions every year to charity. He chose the profession where the road is open, the ladder is up, and the sky is the limit for a salesperson with a creative imagination and a good work ethic!

create a product above your garage one night and sell it on the other side of the world the next day! You couldn't do that when I was a kid.

You Are NOT Stuck In Your Profession

Get over the idea that because you have some kind of professional degree that you need to be stuck in that profession forever. If it is something you are not excited or passionate about and want more out of life, *then choose selling*.

Why?

> *The highest price paid for any form of ability in the world is a master salesperson with a creative imagination!*

With selling, the door is always open, the ladder is always up, and the sky is the limit!

When I started selling life insurance, I was inexperienced, which was part of the reason why 56 insurance companies didn't want to hire me. But I knew I could do this. I was hungry and would not be denied!

When the 57th company finally gave me a chance, I started out slowly with a 1-in-13 closing sales average. By daily taking action, learning and getting better, I lowered my sales average and increased my sales commissions … DRAMATICALLY!

The millions, tens of millions, and hundreds of millions of dollars that I've made in sales since that time have come as a direct result of becoming a master sales person with a creative imagination.

Patricia Moore and her husband left careers of real estate and law enforcement to join a direct selling company. Today they say, "There is no comparison between the money we are currently making and the money we used to make. We now make more in two months than we used to make in a whole year!" Only in selling!

You can do the same if you stop what you are doing and **choose selling**.

It Is NOT Rocket Science!

Companies don't need to hire people with double majors to get the results they want, no matter what they say and no matter what the job description says.

Every company in every part of the world in every language needs one thing!

They need more salespeople!

WHEN do they need them?

Right now!

The full-scale demand for people who can sell is skyrocketing! It's going through the roof! And the pay and commission checks should be going right along with it!

That is a very good thing. This is the time to choose selling!
WHY is the need so strong?

Because nothing happens until somebody sells something.

Every company understands that because every company is at the mercy of its ability to sell. Growth, profits, return on investment, it all comes into play.

At age 25, Mark O. Haroldsen was broke. He had just lost his job and his wife was expecting their second child. Though he borrowed money from his in-laws to pay his bills, he did not give up his dream of becoming a million-aire. He chose selling as his career and has since made tens of millions from his real estate deals!

It is not complicated. It is not rocket science. It is simple. The businesses of the world need salespeople who can sell!

What Is Needed Most

You may remember the days when Magic Johnson played basketball for the Lakers or when he retired in 1991 from the sport because he was infected with HIV, but have you heard from him since?

A lot of people haven't. They probably assumed he was a "has been," destined to disappear into oblivion. **But that's not what happened to Magic Johnson.**

He traded in his basketball shoes for business shoes! **In all respects, he became salesman ... and a good one at that!**

His company, Magic Johnson Enterprises, began by selling companies on doing business in the inner city. Instead of leaving money on the table, Magic saw a need and sold the right people on filling it.

Today, a brief snapshot of his enterprise would include, among other things:
- More than 110 Starbucks
- More than 30 Burger Kings
- More than 10 fitness gyms

He knew what he was doing, he could sell, and his empire is estimated to be worth in excess of $700 million!

Why wouldn't the businesses go into the areas of town that he did and simply do business themselves? "They were scared," Magic says.

> Brothers, Mike and Steve Melia, used to drive a little compact car to their sales appointments ... when they didn't have to push it. They had almost no money, but they had big goals. Today, both are enjoying freedom and six-figure incomes because they mastered selling.

"Scared they were going to lose money. They didn't know how to do business in these communities so they just said, 'We don't need the headache.' And they went elsewhere."

Magic knew what was needed most: someone who could sell, and he chose to be that salesperson.

With more than $3.2 trillion in total revenues, the top 200 U.S. manufacturing firms employ nearly 500,000 sales people. The average annual sales per salesperson at these companies is $6.6 million.

Strong, confident, and smart, Magic sold himself to business owners, investors, and communities.

He sold Sony on opening movie theaters in South Central Los Angeles and Harlem. He sold Starbucks CEO Howard Schultz on a different approach to furthering their business together. And he has sold many other businesses on investing into communities that were previously ignored.

Though Magic does business in more than 80 cities and more than 20 states, it is just the beginning for him! He is a master salesman who knows exactly what is needed most: **more salespeople**.

That is because:

>**People who can sell are in hot demand.**

>**People who gain the ability to sell will always have a job.**

>**People who master selling will be the ones who write the checks.**

Become a master salesperson!

Nigel Chanakira, CEO of Kingdom Meikles Africa Ltd. in Zimbabwe, came from a very humble background, but once introduced to the SMI programs, he learned to set goals and then to sell his way to their achievement. He is now the CEO of the largest conglomerate in Zimbabwe and has business interests across Africa. Nigel has only just begun his selling career!

What Is Needed Most

Chapter Four:
Summary

1. **Every company, charity, profession, and business needs more good salespeople.** There simply can never be enough salespeople, because there is always room for more growth, more sales, and more work.

2. **There has never been a greater time to be a salesperson.** The opportunities are endless, especially with the technological advances of today.

3. **You do not need to be stuck in your profession forever just because you have a degree in it.** If it is something you are not excited or passionate about and want more out of life, then choose selling!

4. **The highest price paid for any form of ability in the world is a master salesperson with a creative imagination.** With selling, the door is always open, the ladder is always up, and the sky is the limit.

5. **People who gain the ability to sell will always have a job; they are in hot demand.** Every company is at the mercy of its ability to sell. Remember, nothing happens until somebody sells something.

**With selling, the door is
always open, the ladder
is always up, and the
sky is the limit!**

Chapter Five

The Sky Is The Limit

There are no limits to how high you can go!

Lee Iacocca displayed his passion for selling at a young age. When he was 10 years old, he would take his wagon to the grocery store and wait outside. As shoppers came out, he would offer to pull their groceries home for them for a tip. By the time he was 16, he worked eight hours a day in a fruit market.

He used his youthful charm and inventive selling skills to get what he wanted.

Hired as an engineer by the Ford Motor Company, he quickly proved that he was better suited for sales. In a career that spanned 40 years, **Iacocca's** maverick, street-smart, "thinking-on-your-feet" approach induced breakthrough programs at Ford, such as the 56-56, a program which made it possible to purchase a new 1956 Ford for 20% down and $56.00 a month for three years.

The program was a huge success. His district went from last place in sales to first place. Due to this program it was estimated that an extra 75 million cars were sold. His creative selling skills were beginning to be noticed.

> She isn't called "The First Lady of American Magazines" for nothing. Cathleen Black, President of Hearst Magazines, can sell! Widely credited for the success of *USA Today*, she began her career in advertising sales. No surprise that a salesperson is at the helm.

Another legendary project that **Iacocca** undertook was the Fairlane Committee, the end product of which was the 1964 Mustang. It was this project that put him on the international platform and gave the world a glimpse of his marketing and management style.

His use of market research, his willingness to listen and his readiness to take risks introducing new products made him a strong business force. **Iacocca**, now known to some as the "Father of the Mustang," was made President of Ford on December 10, 1970.

In 1979 he joined forces with Chrysler and advanced to the position of CEO. Chrysler, having accumulated a huge inventory of low-mileage cars at a time of rising fuel prices, faced bankruptcy. There was a serious lack of communication, and there was no teamwork. Each department seemed to be working in a vacuum.

He had to make some drastic decisions; he was forced to fire many of the executives. Iacocca used his charm and sales skills to ask the federal government for aid, gambling that it would not allow Chrysler to fail when the national economy was already depressed.

Although his sales presentation sparked intense debate over the role of government in a market economy, Congress in 1980 agreed to guarantee $1.5 billion in loans if the company could raise another $2 billion on its own. By 1983, **Iacocca** had Chrysler back on their feet, and on July 13, 1983 Chrysler paid back all their government loans. He made a public statement, "We at Chrysler borrow money the old fashioned way. We pay it back."

What a bold statement! **He was selling confidence, integrity, and trust.** And people were hungry for it!

Harland C. Stonecipher believed in his vision of "justice for all" and sold that vision until it became a reality. His company, Pre-Paid Legal Services, Inc., has changed the industry and has provided an opportunity for its sales force to make hundreds of millions of dollars.

The whole deal succeeded for one reason: his ability to sell.

Positive Expectancy

Lee Iacocca was success-minded, he had a success consciousness and awareness, and he attacked obstacles with positive expectancy. *Positive expectation comes from a sincere, no-limitations belief in conditions and circumstances.* He simply refused to be limited in any way, shape, or form!

Top salespeople possess the same positive expectancy, and so can you!

- **You will wake up each day figuring out ways things can be done instead of thinking of ways they cannot be done.**

- **You will look to your strengths instead of your weaknesses, your power instead of your problems.**

- **You will see potential and possibilities you couldn't see previously.**

- **You will be a much better listener; you will be understood.**

- **Your decision-making faculties will be clearer, and your judgment will be both fair and discerning.**

- **You will enter the arena of life with greater dignity, greater confidence, and greater pride.**

Responsible for all the global business operations for Internet giant, Yahoo, Sue Decker must continually sell. But that isn't hard, because she is a master saleswoman. In 2007, she was promoted again, and this time to President. Whatever her position or title, Sue Decker is sure to impress with her ability to sell.

You also will magnetize the condition you seek through the Law of Attraction, which operates with mathematical certainty.

We attract what we think. Every positive thought has a positive result.

Whatever you vividly imagine, ardently desire, sincerely believe, and enthusiastically act upon … must inevitably come to pass.

Positive thoughts are the basis for success attitudes and success habits, both leading to a positive expectancy in everything we do … especially in selling!

Success Principles of Selling:

Despite what we hear around us, about someone being "lucky" to get a promotion or someone "accidentally" winning a contest, the truth is this: **success is never by accident or luck**.

Real sales success depends on how much of your potential you develop and use. There is no luck or accident involved.

The simplest definition of success is this: *The progressive realization of worthwhile, pre-determined personal goals.*
And consider these principles:

- **Successful sales people make just as many mistakes as anyone else. The only difference is that they learn from their mistakes rather than give up.**

- **The measure of success in selling is what you are doing compared to your true potential.**

"Going into professional sales is one of the best decisions I have made in my life," says William Cham, Master Licensee with Leadership Management Singapore. "It gives me the greatest opportunity to have on-going personal growth, freedom, and financial gain. The sky is the limit for my life and my income!"

- **Focus on one day at a time. Strive mightily, learn wisely, cultivate understanding, and reach for your highest sales goal. Then, tomorrow, repeat what you did today and, as sure as day follows night, your sales will increase and so will your income.**

Truly successful sales people are willing to be a leader to others. They are not restricted by the way "things have always been done." Their leadership is a continuing search for the best way, not the most familiar. Our nation possesses thousands of potential sales leaders.

Highly successful sales people have all found a way to develop a decisive, well-developed plan that uses all their sales strengths and abilities to their maximum potential.

By focusing on one day at a time, you can begin the exciting journey of fulfilling your own personal sales goals and dreams.

You will come to believe, as I have, the powerful truth of these words: *"Whatever you vividly imagine, ardently desire, sincerely believe, and enthusiastically act upon ... must inevitably come to pass!"* Start today!

Only In Sales

Only in sales can you start at the bottom of a company and rise to the top. How is that possible? What does the most junior salesperson — *who becomes a great salesperson* — have that the receptionist, accountant, or manager does not have?

The answer is simple!

The great salesperson has the qualities necessary to be successful and to be the leader. Interestingly, only through selling do you get those qualities.

> No doubt you have heard that some people can "take a lemon and turn it into lemonade." Those words describe a salesperson perfectly. One great example is Martha Stewart. She spent time in jail ... and bounced right back. She can sell!

And wouldn't you agree that the person running a company needs to be the one who has those specific qualities? You can always hire accountants, lawyers, managers, and employees, but you want a president, a key leader in the company, to also be a master salesperson.

You are not alone in your answer. That is precisely why salespeople rise through the ranks to run multi-million dollar and multi-billion dollar companies. Only a good salesperson could handle it!

Pharmaceutical sales is expected to grow nearly 28% in the decade between 2004 and 2014, making it one of the hottest sales industries according to the U.S. Department of Labor. They need all the sales-people they can get.

And only in sales can you reach any height you choose. The sky is the limit!

From Ho-Hum To Great!

Not only do good sales people possess the unusual ability to rise to the top, they can also take an average ho-hum opportunity and turn it into a phenomenal success.

How? Because they can sell! I have seen countless times how one good salesperson can boost sales in a business that is located in an area of town that seem unsuited for success. The only explanation … a master salesperson is at work!

I personally took a business that was on its way toward bankruptcy and increased sales by 1,500%! Years later, the business was sold for millions of dollars, but if I had not boosted sales, the company couldn't have been given away. **That's another reason that companies need more good salespeople!**

Though she has a master's degree in biology/ biochemistry and a MBA in finance, it was her ability to sell that elevated Christine Poon to the position of Vice Chairman of powerhouse Johnson & Johnson.

Remember, **nothing happens until you sell something.** With stellar sales, a great salesperson can take even one-half of a good idea and do incredibly well.

Unlimited Horizons

Selling is a profession that represents an unlimited horizon without restrictions. To the young man or woman planning their personal future, a career in sales provides practical experience, personal satisfaction, and incredible income potential.

Just one company, Avon, has an estimated 5 million salespeople in the U.S. selling Avon Products ... and they could use 5 million more!

Selling is an exciting and rewarding career and a *good salesperson is a skilled craftsman.* I think I can best illustrate this point by citing the aptitudes we seek in potential representatives for our own organization, Success Motivation International, Inc.

We look for evidence of the following key abilities:

- **Communication ...** The ability to present our products and services with words.

- **Motivation ...** The perceptive ability to understand a customer's needs, wants, and desires.

- **Self-Confidence ...** The ability to generate and sustain enthusiasm.

- **Perseverance ...** The emotional and moral stamina to persist regardless of frustrations and temporary defeats.

- **Determination ...** The ability to close the sale.

Phil Knight, the co-founder and former CEO of Nike, Inc., built a successful business by selling shoes and a billionaire by selling dreams!

Naturally, we don't find all of these qualities fully developed in every prospective salesperson, but more often than not, we do find a definite propensity, sincerity, and honest desire to learn.

Selling is a profession that represents an unlimited horizon without restrictions!

And that is where you start! Over time, master salespeople possess these very skills, and those skills are worth millions, and even billions, of dollars!

To the curious who ask, *"Just what is a salesperson?"* I say:

- **First**, salespeople are schooled in their specialty, have undergone intensive training, understand the product, and how they can best serve those who buy it.

- **Second**, salespeople never stop learning. They maintain a consistent and continuing program of self-improvement with the sole purpose of providing better service.

- **Third**, salespeople understand and practice the rewarding science of motivation. They motivate their customers for their greater benefit and they motivate themselves to continued accomplishment.

- **Fourth,** salespeople are dedicated to maintaining the highest standards of their profession.

- **Fifth,** salespeople realize that their continuing success is dependent upon the confidence and goodwill of other people. They consider this trust their finest possession and greatest asset.

Joe Girard is recognized by the Guinness Book of World Records as the most successful car salesman, selling 13,001 cars at a Chevrolet dealership in Detroit. He overcame a troubled youth to fine-tune his intense passion to sell. As a result, he set consecutives sales records over a 15-year period. He was a master salesman!

The successful salesperson differs radically from his or her unsuccessful counterpart principally because they are ***completely dominated by success thinking.***

Everyone has but one mind, and that mind can be dominated by either success or failure. Remember this psychological truth: a single mind cannot be divided against itself. ***It's impossible, no matter how hard you try, to think of failure in one direction and success in the other.***

When you remove all limitations and see the sky as your limit, you have discovered what I call "success blinders." Let those success blinders keep you from seeing all reasons why you shouldn't, couldn't, or wouldn't do what you want to do.

Then go do it! You can!

The Sky Is The Limit!

More than 2 million women in North America now make Curves a part of their regular weekly routine. There are an estimated 10,000 outlets open in the US and Canada. Currently, one in every four health clubs in the country is a Curves for Women, and hundreds more are under construction. The company also has opened centers in six other countries.

Not bad at all for a man who dropped out of college to chase a dream. **Gary Heavin** left medical school after just two years because of an entrepreneurial itching within him.

> **He wanted to be an owner.**

> **He wanted to control his own destiny.**

When Fran Alexander's husband got sick with cancer, she took time off from work. And when he died, she took more time off. All told, she was not working for three years. During that time, her high six-figure income continued! Only in selling can you create residual income that pays you, even when you are not at work!

He wanted to chase something that mattered to him.

He wanted a business where he could use his creative sales skills.

He wanted to sell.

In 1995, he and his wife **Diane** came up with a creative way for women to exercise, and Curves for Women was born! He chose to focus on the "average" woman, providing an atmosphere that fostered camaraderie, encouragement, exercise, and a healthy lifestyle, all for a very reasonable price.

Positions for retail salespersons are projected to increase by over 17%, to nearly 5 million, between 2004 and 2014.

Gary hired the best franchise salespeople he could find and the business took off. Franchises began to sell like hotcakes! Now, a multi-millionaire many times over, **Gary** and **Diane** continue to expand the reaches of Curves, adding country after country as they span the globe.

This husband and wife team did it with creative selling!

Entrepreneur magazine described Curves as the fastest-growing franchise in the world. Gary and Diane Heavin did it with selling, selling, and more selling!

The Sky Is The Limit

Chapter Five:
Summary

1. **Top salespeople possess positive expectancy.** This quality comes from a sincere, no-limitations belief in conditions and circumstances.

2. **The Law of Attraction states that we attract what we think.** Every positive thought has a positive result. Positive thoughts are the basis for success attitudes and success habits.

3. **Success is never by accident or luck; real sales success depends on how much of your potential you develop and use.** The definition of success is, "The progressive realization of worthwhile, pre-determined personal goals."

4. **Truly successfully salespeople are not restricted by the way things have always been done.** Instead, they are continually searching for the best way, not the most familiar.

5. **Highly successful salespeople have all found a way to create a decisive, well-developed plan that uses all their sales strengths and abilities to their maximum potential.** Remember this: "Whatever you vividly imagine, ardently desire, sincerely believe, and enthusiastically act upon … must inevitably come to pass!"

6. **Only in sales can you start at the bottom of a company and rise to the top.** Selling is a profession that represents an unlimited horizon without restrictions. The sky is the limit!

7. **What is a salesperson?** A salesperson is always well-trained, never stops learning, practices the science of motivation, is dedicated to maintaining the highest standards of selling, and considers trust the greatest asset.

When you are in selling,
you can go make it happen,
whenever you want.
You have the power to
reach your dreams!

Chapter Six

"Hello, Golden Opportunity!"

Selling is your ticket to a successful, prosperous future!

The son of Russian immigrants, **Bernard Rapoport** was born in 1917 in San Antonio, Texas. Although he felt loved and nurtured, his youth was marred by the family's grinding poverty and the many humiliations it caused. For a number of years, he never experienced having the lights, phone, gas, and water all turned on at the same time.

After a series of low-paying jobs and financial setbacks, **Rapoport** *took a job selling* insurance for the Pioneer American Insurance Company of Houston. Within a few months he moved to Waco, Texas, and opened a general agency office, which quickly became a success.

"I learned that genuine, sincere, enthusiasm is contagious," says **Rapoport**, who had finally found his niche. A year later, an uncle

---

Only in selling can you go from the bottom to the top! Pam Nicholson, now the EVP and COO of Enterprise Rent-A-Car, started in 1981 behind the rental counter! She rose to the top because of her passion for customer service and her incredible ability to sell.

---

asked **Rapoport** to go in with him on an insurance company in Indiana. He borrowed $25,000 and founded the American Income Life Insurance Company in 1951, which quickly grew nationwide.

In 1994, after more than four decades guiding and growing his company, **Rapoport** sold it to Torchmark Corporation. Aware of how critical **Rapoport's** leadership had been to the company's success, the acquisition agreement included keeping him on as chairman and CEO.

Insurance is big business in the U.S. The top 10 companies with the largest sales teams generate more than $97 billion in sales and employ approximately 437,000 salespeople in the U.S. They can use thousands more!

A thread that has run true throughout **Rapoport's** life is his sense of responsibility. He worked as a youngster to help his family, he supported his sister throughout her college years, and he devoted himself to making his company one of the most successful insurance businesses in the nation.

Bernard Rapoport chose selling, and as a result, he was able to accomplish his goals and dreams.

Was It Worth It?

You bet it was worth it! At the tune of $100 million, I would say it was certainly worth it.

Many others, like **Bernard Rapoport**, had creative ideas and went on to become incredibly successful … because they could sell. Whether

Austrian-born sales trainer and successful publisher Gerhard Gschwandtner is the founder of the highest-circulation, and possibly the most influential, sales magazine in the world, *Selling Power*. He seems to have mastered what his magazine stands for: selling!

they were selling their ideas, their story, or their vision, they were selling!

A new idea will drive you to great heights, but expect to be hit by those who oppose you, don't like you, or are intimidated by you.

Be ready! Expect it. It is actually a good thing!

And that is where negative capability comes in.

U.S. workers were recently surveyed and 50% responded that they intended to seek a new job. The greatest opportunity for this group would be in selling!

Negative Capability = Positive Expectancy

The term "negative capability" was coined by an English poet, John Keats. Keats' definition of negative capability: "… that is when a man is capable of being in uncertainties, mysteries, doubts without any irritable reaching after fact and reason."

I first heard of negative capability years ago while in Singapore, while attending a luncheon with a very successful businessman, Mr. Wong. I was especially intrigued when he arrived at lunch in a chauffer driven Rolls Royce limousine. I wanted to find out what this guy was made of — what made him tick?

So I asked him, what is the one characteristic, if he had to pick only one, that he felt accounted for his great success. I was astonished by his answer. Do you know what he said?

He looked at me for just a second and then said, **"The key factor of my success has been my negative capability."**

Ellen Kullman's team brings in 45% of the company's $27 billion revenue. Starting in 1988 as a marketing manager at DuPont, she was named EVP in 2006. Prior to DuPont, Kullman worked for General Electric in various business, marketing, and sales positions. Clearly, she is a master saleswoman … and clearly, the sky is the limit!

That was the first time I had ever heard the phrase. When I asked him what negative capability meant, he explained it this way:

> *"It is the ability to bounce back from failure, to overcome obstacles, and to take a calculated risk."*

In other words …

you waste no time in worry,

not a second in doubt,

no time wasted in frustration, and

don't even wonder why you faced the obstacles.

To him, it was an assumption that he would face the obstacles. He was not caught off guard or surprised. He expected the obstacles to come.

You certainly cannot be surprised when someone gives you an objection in a sale; most people think of the objection in the sale is a negative. However, it's not a negative because you couldn't make the sale if you didn't get some objections. Often times, all they want is more information.

Mr. Wong emphasized the importance of focusing on positive possibilities for overcoming objections. **Basically, you refuse to allow the negative forces in the environment to control you or your emotions.**

Estée Lauder, using selling, transformed beauty into big business that controls 45% of the cosmetics market in U.S. department stores that sells in 118 countries and in 2006 grew to be $3.6 billion in sales. She started her enterprise by selling skin creams concocted by her uncle, a chemist, in beauty shops, beach clubs and resorts. No doubt the potions were good — but the saleslady was better. She simply outsold everyone else in the cosmetics industry!

When The Going Gets Tough …

Have you ever thought to yourself: "This year has been one of the worst years in my life!" Many of us probably have, but remember you can always strive to make the next year your best if you don't quit!

I set a goal one year to sell a million dollars of insurance in a year. To some people my goal seemed like such a fantasy —

It is estimated that in the decade from 2004 to 2014 the insurance sales industry will grow by 23.1%. More opportunities for choosing selling!

so far away and out of reach! Well, I knew the trouble I had even getting the job selling insurance, being rejected by 50 some odd companies. Still I felt, well, I'm going to do it in a year.

I put all of these things down in my goal setting. I sure didn't want to share them with anyone, but this is what I had in my goals book.

- I was going to sell $1 million worth of insurance in a year,
- Then I was going to do it in six months,
- Then I was going to do it in three months,
- Then I was going to do it in a month,
- Then I was going to do it in a week, and
- **Then I was one day going to do it in <u>one day</u>!**

I sold a million that first year in 1950, after I had changed from a weekly premium debit to ordinary insurance. The next year in 1951, I sold a million in six months.

> Joshua Denne, fresh out of jail and without a high school diploma, was sweeping the floors at a machine shop, but he wanted more. When he was introduced to selling, he found what he was looking for. Today, he has financial freedom … and the car of his dreams, the house of his dreams, and much more. He chose selling!

The next year during 1952, there was a period of three months that I sold a million; in 1953, I sold that in a month. Yes, in 1954, I sold a million in a week and then in a day! (In today's dollars, that would be more than $12,000,000!)

As the need for professional services such as accounting and tax planning increases, so will the need for a sales force to promote these services. From 2004 to 2014, it is estimated that this segment of the sales industry will increase by 50%. They cannot do it without sales people!

So what was impossible back in 1949 as a sure fantasy dream to do in a year, I later did in just one day. I'm not trying to boast about something I did. The only reason I am sharing that with you is to show you that from your position now, you can go to the absolute top of any mountain if you choose selling!

Stick with it. Learn each day and grow. The world can be your oyster!

Overcoming Negative Circumstances

No matter how strong your positive mental attitude, there are times when you are surrounded by negative people at work, at home, or anywhere else.

You can even be careful about the friends you choose, but you are still going to end up dealing with people who tell you to not go into selling.

That's just the way it is, ***but don't let that detour you!***

This is your chance to choose the best route to success. This is your chance to overcome unanticipated obstacles, to hear discouraging opinions, and to go forward … ***and to stay focused until you reach your sales goal!***

> Incredibly, it was a mouse that put Walt Disney on the map, but it was his ability to sell that brought him fame and fortune.

Many people reach unanticipated obstacles and they quit. They see the obstacle as an impassable roadblock. They give up. They may be only three feet from gold! They just need to dig a little deeper because 90% of all failure comes from quitting!

But this is where you excel. This is where you take it to the top. This is where you take the lead all the way to the finish line because nothing, no one, can stop you on your destined path to become a master salesperson.

Negative Capability Is An Absolute Necessity

Bill Cosby is a classic example of someone who has found negative capability a very valuable tool in achieving phenomenal success. He grew up poor in the slums of Philadelphia. **Cosby's** father was an alcoholic, who later deserted the family, and his mother was a scrubwoman.

However, he didn't let these negatives affect or stand in his way in order to use them for excuses. Cosby was persistent and turned his negatives into positives; he had negative capability.

Another rags to riches success story is **Dave Thomas**, the founder of Wendy's Restaurant, who started out as a dishwasher. With a lot of hard work and determination, Wendy's became the third largest hamburger chain in the country. **Dave Thomas** had negative capability.

Negative capability is an absolute necessity. Not every idea will be a hit, not every venture will succeed, and not every goal you set is going to be reached.

Sam Castor didn't finish college and had little business experience, but he could sell. He says, "Being a success is directly equated to your ability to serve others and their needs; those are the opportunities I look for." His first two business ventures failed, but his third, Mannatech, a nutritional supplement company, is doing hundreds of millions in sales today. Sam serves as he sells.

In fact, if none of your plans ever fail, that is a sure sign you are being too conservative. I'm not reckless, but I'm a risk taker—a calculated risk taker.

Still, I have experienced more failures than successes. Honestly I didn't even know that until I sat down one day and listed the companies that I had started (over 100) and figured out how many companies did not work out (over 60). Now, the 40 or so

A 2005 survey conducted at top U.S. companies indicated that the number of sales positions was increasing. Nearly 75% said they anticipated hiring additional external sales representatives. Conversely, approximately 50% said they planned to hire additional internal and web-based sales representatives in the near future.

companies that succeeded have done very well. So to speak, I've hit several grand slams and several home runs, and the results have been millions in cash.

Baseball legend, **Babe Ruth**, was well known for his home runs, but few people know that he also held the record for strikeouts!

Goodbye, Mediocrity … Hello, Golden Opportunity

Nobody has to live a life of mediocrity. Each of us has a harp with a thousand strings. Why would anyone want to use just one string?

Each of us can dip into the rivers of opportunity and of plenty that continually flow around us. Why use a teaspoon to scoop up what is yours when you can use a steam shovel?

Each of us can paint the most amazing of pictures. We have access to all the colors in the rainbow. Why would anyone settle for battleship gray?

Lorna Rasmussen left her degree and the film industry because she wasn't making any money. She chose selling and enjoys both helping other people and her six-figure income.

You have the right to be, do, and accomplish anything that you want.

The world is open before you. It is your golden opportunity.

And my advice is to go after it!

Choose selling.

Hello, Golden Opportunity

Dave Longaberger was born with three strikes against him. His family was poor (there were 12 kids in the family!), he stuttered, and he had epilepsy.

But **Longaberger** would not let his liabilities stand in the way of his ambition. In the early 1970s, he noticed a trend

Multiple surveys have found that 87% of Americans don't like their jobs (Forbes.com). They should get into sales!

— that woven baskets were becoming very popular. He also noticed that many department stores were beginning to sell imported baskets. **Longaberger** wondered if people would appreciate baskets like the fine handcrafted ones his father used to make.

Acting on the creative impulse, he asked his father, J.W., to make a dozen baskets and then took them to a nearby town. **He sold them immediately and the shop requested more!**

J.W. made several dozen more baskets. Sadly, however, he died at the age of 71 just as the family trade was being renewed.

Longaberger opened J.W.'s Handwoven Baskets in 1976 in Dresden, Ohio. Sales of the handmade baskets increased to the point that he had to find a place to expand his small basket factory.

> Steve Jobs introduces the iPod and sales of this Apple product go through the roof! That is what happens when you combine sales ability with a creative imagination!

He found an old mill (built in the 1890s) that had been vacant for over 20 years. Though it had broken windows, uneven floors, and a sagging roof, **Longaberger** envisioned a basket factory with hundreds of craftsmen and craftswomen weaving, tacking, talking, and laughing. With great enthusiasm, he pursued his vision. **He knew he could sell the baskets.**

Over time, he became increasingly convinced that American consumers wanted the handmade craftsmanship and quality of Longaberger baskets. He tried selling baskets at malls, department stores, and other retails outlets, but had limited success.

A recent survey indicated that 96% of employees leave current positions because they are seeking a higher income opportunity. However, 44% look for new opportunities because they believe the possibilities for growth in their current positions are very limited.

In 1978, he discovered that the most effective way to sell the company's baskets was through home shows where someone with knowledge of Longaberger baskets would share the history and explain the craftsmanship that each basket holds. *The company's direct sales organization was born.*

In 1984, his daughter, **Tami**, joined the company full-time after her graduation from college. **Tami** worked in virtually every area of the company, and in 1994 she became company president. Working side by side until **Dave's** death in 1999, **Tami** learned her father's sales method first-hand.

Master sales trainer, author and speaker Tom Hopkins said, "Believe me, when I got into sales, I had too much month at the end of the money." After benefiting from professional training, he became a dedicated student, internalizing and refining sales techniques that enabled him to become the sales leader in his industry and the world's greatest sales trainer!

Under **Tami's** leadership, customers have developed an amazing passion for baskets. The company has been featured for its cutting edge employee programs and outstanding corporate citizenship. His younger daughter, **Rachel**, carries on the family's tradition of philanthropy by heading The Longaberger Foundation, which has donated millions to local charities and educational institutions since its inception in 1998.

Today, Longaberger is America's premier maker of handcrafted baskets and offers other home and lifestyle products, including pottery, wrought iron, fabric accessories, and specialty foods.

In addition, there are more than 60,000 independent Home Consultants (salespeople) located in all states of the US who sell Longaberger products directly to customers.

Not bad at all for a man who started out poor, stuttered, and had epilepsy! The point is, it doesn't matter who you are, where you were born, or what you look like. **The world of selling is available to all and everyone!**

Seize the day! If opportunity knocks, choose selling. And if it's not knocking at your door, go out and look for it! Thousands of companies need salespeople, or create your own ideas and sell it. The main thing is for you to remember (memorize):

> **"The highest price paid for any form of ability in the world is a master salesperson with a creative imagination."**

Darnell Self sold clothes in a mall, but he was capable of much more. He knew selling was the vehicle, but wasn't sure which company would have the key to success. He found the right company and his true capabilities blossomed. He worked diligently to grow his business, has helped many other people reach their financial dreams, and was named the "Entrepreneur of the Year" by the National Black Chamber of Commerce. He has come a long way from working in a mall. Today, he earns over $1,000,000 a year in selling!

"Hello, Golden Opportunity!"

Chapter Six:
Summary

1. **Negative capability is key to sales success.** It is the ability to bounce back from failure, to overcome obstacles, and to take a calculated risk. Top sales people refuse to allow the negative forces in their environment to control them or their emotions.

2. **No matter how strong your positive mental attitude, there are times when you are surrounded by negative people.** Don't let that detour you or consider quitting. Stay focused until you reach your goals; ninety percent of all failure comes from quitting.

3. **Not every idea will be a hit, not every venture will succeed, and not every goal you set is going to be reached.** If none of your plans ever fail, that is a sure sign you are being too conservative. Be a calculated risk taker.

4. **Nobody has to live a life of mediocrity.** You have the right to be, do, and accomplish anything that you want. The world is open before you – it is your golden opportunity!

5. **The world of selling is available to everyone.** If opportunity knocks, choose selling. And if it's not knocking at your door, go out and look for it.

Whatever you vividly imagine,
ardently desire, sincerely believe,
and enthusiastically act upon ...
must inevitably come to pass.

Chapter Seven

Stay In Charge

A home-based business places
you in the driver's seat!!

Cell-culture technology may not be glamorous, but it interested **Dr. Myron Wentz**. He wanted to help people in the area of health, and in 1974 he founded Gull Laboratories. His small one-man operation went on to become the world's leading producer of commercially available diagnostic test kits for viruses.

The product was great and it was easy to sell. He had plenty of passionate belief.

But **Dr. Wentz** wanted to prevent diseases rather than detect them. He knew that environment, lifestyle, and diet played an important part in good health, but it was the impact of antioxidants in countering the negative effect of "free radicals" in the human body that really got his interest. (Free radicals are believed to be the cause of many degenerative diseases.)

Wayne Root wanted to be a sports analyst on TV, but he had no experience, no training, no degree, and no contacts. His vision to be in charge fueled his passion. Wayne went on to become the sports analyst he dreamed of, and also a speaker, author, trainer, and multi-millionaire. He took charge and sold his way to the top!

Dr. Wentz wanted to do more and to be more. **He wanted to be in charge.** He wanted his work to help prevent rather than only detect disease. **He wanted people to be in control of their own lives.**

So, after many years of research, study, breakthroughs, and success, **Dr. Wentz** — an internationally recognized microbiologist, immunologist, and pioneer in the development of human cell culture technology and infectious disease diagnoses — *jumped ship!*

According to Entrepreneur.com, there were 13.8 million income-generating home-based businesses in 2005, and the number continues to climb.

He sold his controlling interests in Gull Laboratories in 1992 and founded USANA Health Sciences, a state-of-the-art manufacturer of vitamin and nutritional supplements.

He jumped completely into selling!

Dr. Wentz argues that he is first and foremost a scientist, not a businessman or a salesman, but his talents in business and in selling are evident. He was appointed as an advisor to the Small Business Administration and in 2003 was the recipient of the Utah Ernst & Young Entrepreneur of the Year award.

And in the area of selling, Usana Health Sciences took off!

Today, USANA reports: "Usana products are on the leading edge of providing adequate cell-level nutrition, fiber, and antioxidant protection

---

When his mother died tragically from unsafe dieting practices, young Mark Hughes vowed to find a way to help people lose weight safely. He studied the time-honored practice of using herbs for improving health in China, then returned to the US and in 1980 launched Herbalife. His passion and enthusiasm spread, as did Herbalife products. Today, Herbalife is a billion-dollar business with more than 1.5 million sales associates in 60+ countries worldwide. Mark could sell!

---

for our bodies. **Dr. Wentz** is applying the same level of scientific expertise, technical brilliance, and dedication he employed in pioneering viral diagnostics to create breakthrough approaches to nutritional wellness."

USANA Health Sciences, Inc., is a direct selling company. **Dr. Wentz** created a home-based business opportunity for tens of thousands of people! These independent Associates distribute and sell scientifically based nutritional supplements and personal-care products. **Net sales for USANA Health Sciences in the year 2008 were over $420 million.** USANA Health Services operates in more than a dozen countries worldwide.

In addition to USANA Health Sciences, **Dr. Wentz** created Sanoviv Medical Institute, a holistic medical facility with full hospital accreditation located in Baja California.

In everything Dr. Wentz does, he is selling, and he's in charge!

Get In Charge, Stay In Charge

For many, the best way to take advantage of the opportunity that selling presents is to start with a home-based business. No where else is the ground more fertile for making your dreams come true than through the art of direct selling within a home-based business.

A home-based business places **you**, and no one but **you**, completely in the driver's seat of your life!

In fact, recent estimates show that as many as 20% of all new small businesses are operated directly out of the home. And those businesses

> After college, Darren Hitz was frustrated, trying to figure out what he wanted to do. The idea of a shuttle service for bachelor parties led to the idea of bachelor adventures, and Adventure Bachelor Party was born. He chose selling and found his niche!

are a true testament to the entrepreneurial spirit, *generating more than $100 billion in annual revenue! Yes, that's 100 <u>BILLION</u> dollars!*

What other circumstance allows you to set your own work schedule, plan time for a full social life, and experience ultimate flexibility to meet family obligations at the same time and with unlimited reward? There is *no other circumstance!*

With your own home-based business there is:

- **No boss** to report to … you are the boss!
- **No rigid work hours** … you decide when to start & when to stop.
- **No aggravating office politics** … you choose whether to work alone or include others.
- **No financial ceiling** ... you set the salary you want to make.
- **No conflict between work and family** … you stay in control of how your time is spent.

Begin Right Where You Are

Regardless of education level, social status, color, sex, age, or size, what is important is your burning desire to succeed and the perseverance to set your sails and *refuse to give up* until you see your goals fully realized.

Success is entirely up to you. You're the one that decides. You're the one in charge!

World-renowned comedian and actor Bill Cosby has a great desire for success. From his humble beginning, he knew that his desire for success should be greater than his fear of failure. He never let obstacles stand in his way as he sold himself to the world!

The Benefits of a Home-Based Business

BENEFIT #1 — Personal freedom

The greatest benefit to a home-based business is the *personal freedom* you can exercise over you own life. Not a small thing!

- **YOU** choose what type of business opportunity suits you best.
- **YOU** shape your day-to-day work hours in anyway you choose.
- **YOU** decide how far up the success ladder you wish to go.

Home-based businesses allow maximum flexibility for adjusting to the needs of your individual life and family.

Parents can be available to their children after school or to attend special school events or conferences.

If you have never been a morning person, and yet can be incredibly productive as day continues into evening, a home-based business allows your night owl personality to thrive.

There are no corporate rules to helm you in or slow you down. There is no "water cooler gossip" to impede or derail your climb to the top… no one to report to or please.

You're in the driver's seat!

Alexander Elder, M.D., one of today's leading experts on stock trading and a best-selling author, sold his way into his profession. At age 23, he jumped a Soviet Union ship and received political asylum in the US. He worked as a psychiatrist, but found his calling in the psychology of trading. He took charge by selling his insights to the financial world.

BENEFIT #2 — **Reduce your stress**

Just knowing you are in charge of your own life and schedule can minimize your stress level tremendously. And a home-based business provides the perfect avenue for stress control. As long as you have focus and can get the work done you need to, it doesn't matter *when* you actually do it!

Despise that early morning commute? Skip it when you set your own schedule. ***Start the day when you are ready.***

Need time off for dental appointments or to coordinate vacation days with your spouse or "just because?" ***Take it; your time is your own***.

Daycare costs eating up a large percentage of your present salary? ***Stay home with your kids and put that money toward expanding your own business or meeting family needs.***

Lowering your stress is a tremendous benefit ... and it's a great feeling!

BENEFIT #3 — **Include your family**

Many couples or families decide to work together in a particular business that uses their collective talents and skills. That way they can "spell" each other with child care demands or other family obligations.

Working out of your home is also a great learning opportunity for younger children. They learn first hand the character building skills

---

In 1975, Blair Hull developed an option valuation model that proved to be highly accurate. His lifelong fascination with investing would pay off handsomely as he sold his model to the investment community. Blair founded a trading company in 1985, which he sold to Goldman, Sachs & Co. Staying in charge, Blair launched another business, Matlock Capital, in 1999. The ability to sell knows no bounds!

---

of diligence, focus, personal responsibility, and reward. ***Grown children can be an especially great asset to a family-run, home-based business***.

One famous family business name, **Regal Ware** cookware has become the enthusiastic career choice for *four generations* of the Reigle family. **Jeffrey Reigle**, current company president and chief executive officer, says that family members are his most trusted advisors. **Reigle** says, "I know that they give me their honest opinions and really care about what's going on. Today, my brother and my two sons are part of the business, and my father is chairman of the board."

BENEFIT #4 — Significant financial reward

The only limitation to your total financial freedom is the limitation you impose on yourself. Millions of people are starting, running, and profiting from home-based businesses every day. ***YOU can be one of them!***

A home-based business opens doors for the handicapped, students, homemakers, and others who might have a tougher time of landing the usual corporate positions to have unlimited access to financial reward.

Conducting business from home eliminates the high overhead costs of operating a window-front store or office. ***You can pour all those savings directly back into your own operation, allowing you to expand your own business at greater speed!***

Your earning potential is no longer controlled. You do not have to hope for or beg for a raise. ***Whenever you boost your own revenue, you can give yourself a raise anytime!***

Back in the 1930s, Hubert Hansen thought he found a niche: selling his fresh, non-pasteurized juices to film studios and retailers in Southern California. With the help of his three sons, the Hansen juices began to sell. Over 70 years later, the business is still going strong. Hubert Hansen took charge through selling!

No one understands better than **Robert Kiyosaki**, author of the mega-hit best seller, ***Rich Dad Poor Dad*** what leaving behind the typical 9-to-5 job can do for you. His life and therefore his book challenged all the "old ways" of thinking about how to go about reaching your financial goals ... plans like getting a college education and then

"The No 1 thing people can do to increase their wealth is to start a part-time business."
-Robert Kiyosaki, author of
Rich Dad Poor Dad

working for one company for 30 years and retiring with a pension.

In today's world, Kiyosaki believes working the "old formula" is the ***biggest mistake*** you can make! With corporate mergers and down-sizing happening all the time, not to mention the limitations placed on you by the rules of the corporation, ***your life is in anyone's hands but yours***!

Robert and his wife didn't give up on their dreams when the going got tough. They where even homeless for a time and slept in their old beat up Toyota. They were taunted by those who knew their situation and advised to "just get a *regular* job," but they were determined to set their own course.

They didn't give up and they didn't give out ... they just kept working and believing!

They learned valuable lessons from every obstacle they encountered.

Sam Walton, founder of Wal-Mart, brought low prices to small cities, and as its creator, also changed the way big business is run. Walton began a crusade that lasted the rest of his life: to drive down costs in the stores, in the manufacturing, and with the middlemen. It was not an easy sale, but he sold the idea over and over and over. Selling, selling, selling until he had gained worldwide acceptance for his great idea.

BENEFIT #5 — Increase your competitive edge

Because you are working out of your home, your overhead is drastically reduced. The money you save on overhead can be funneled directly into growing your business!

Lowering your operating costs allows you to be **highly competitive** with other people's products, businesses, and services. You can pass on those competitive advantages to your customers in lower prices and more personal service … all winners in building your customer base!

The best salespeople in the world value their customers. **They don't cut corners and manipulate people to grab the quick sale.** Wise salespeople care about their customers and know they are building a long-term relationship.

Developing a solid life philosophy will give you the underpinnings necessary to building a great life AND a competitive, successful home-based business.

Jim Rohn, business philosopher and author of numerous works over the last 40 years, including **The Five Major Pieces to the Life Puzzle**, says that building your own personal philosophy of life and success is the most crucial *first step* in assuring your goals.

In debt to her eyeballs and hating her job in a large hospital, college-educated Meloni Barkley desperately wanted to be her own boss, to get out of debt, and to live a better life. Her sister invited her to an Arbonne skin care presentation, and Meloni reluctantly went. Unexpectedly, the business opportunity turned out to be exactly what Meloni wanted. Today, Meloni's husband is retired (still in his 30s), they are almost out of dept, and they are about to build their dream home. Meloni took charge of her life when she chose selling.

Finding himself broke at age 25 with no money to care for his family, Rohn met a wealthy entrepreneur, John Earl Shoaff, who became Rohn's employer for five of the most influential years of his life.

Fortune magazine has predicted that between 2006 and 2016, 10 million Americans will become millionaires. "Many will be from the industry of direct selling" the magazine says.

Learning the principles of developing his own philosophy so transformed his life that Rohn became a millionaire by the time he was 31 years old!

Rohn suggests keeping a journal as a way of cataloging your experiences and ideas that allows you to think more objectively about your life. Formulating your own beliefs, a *"creed of life"* so to speak, will keep you anchored and focused. You must continue to observe, learn, and grow in order to be successful in life, not just business.

Expanding your competitive edge by constantly learning new things and keeping yourself motivated is not only crucial, but FUN!!

Exposing yourself to the great life philosophers, thinkers, business gurus, and spiritual mentors through books, tapes, and seminars will fill your life with the necessary knowledge and inspiration to fuel your way to the finish line in *every area* of your life!

The year was 1985 and Tony Little, a then unknown body builder, was trying to create his own personal training TV show. It was a success, but his big break came when he met the President and Founder of Home Shopping Network and they struck a deal: if Tony could sell 400 of his videos in four airings, then they could work together on other projects. It worked; Tony sold all 400 videos in four minutes, and the rest is history. Tony chose to be in charge through selling.

BENEFIT #6 — Greater productivity

When you are the direct beneficiary of your own efforts, your enthusiasm tends to be higher and your productivity greater.

Just eliminating the normal commute and the dictates of other people's needs and agendas frees up more time and energy to further your own goals.

If you recruit others to work on your team, keep in mind that people are motivated by opportunities that are easy, fun, and as lucrative as possible.

The more tools you can give those you recruit, the easier it is for them to do their job and the quicker you'll experience a return on their efforts.

People also love having a good time, so the more **FUN** you can make your business, the longer people will work with you and the **HIGHER YOUR REVENUES** will climb!

And of course, you need to make it lucrative for them, not just you. *The more they earn, the more incentive they have to keep going … and the more everyone benefits!*

BENEFIT #7 — Enjoy tax advantages

Using your home as your main place of business offers you multiple opportunities for tax advantages. And who wouldn't appreciate that!

In 1975, Isamu Masuda had an idea for an invention that he believed would relax and energize millions of people who suffered from sore feet. He set to work, and formed a company that is today at the forefront of the rapidly expanding $200-billion global wellness industry. His company: Nikken. Without question, Isamu Masuda is brilliant, but he can also sell!

What can you deduct?

- A percentage of your mortgage payment or rent, insur ance, utilities, additional phone lines, property taxes, household maintenance, security devices, and repairs … **deduct it!**

- A percentage of your vehicle expenses such as gas, insurance, and depreciation … **deduct it!**

- A portion of your moving expenses to another location … **deduct it!**

- Entertaining a client or prospective client over lunch while talking about business matters … **deduct it!**

- Software used for business purposes … **deduct it!**

- Educational expenses required to learn or supplement your business … **deduct it!**

And much more!

As you can see, there are HUGE advantages tax-wise to a home-based business!

You will need to consult with a tax expert to clarify all the potential deductions you can enjoy and to make sure you are clear about the type of records you will need to keep. (One great book on this topic is *Inc. and Grow Rich*.)

While in language school in Perugia, Italy, Paula Lambert fell in love with fresh mozzarella cheese! Her goal: to offer the same hand-made Italian cheeses back home in Dallas, Texas. From that point forward, Paula was in selling! She thrived, and today The Mozzerella Company is a huge success.

Wrapping It Up!

Keep in mind that *you can start your home-based business at any level* ... part time, full time, in your garage, in a spare room, with help or without, with minimum investment, and a minimum of obligations or risk.

There are literally thousands of home-based businesses already available and looking for you or you can create and promote your own "never-been-done-before" concept. *You decide!*

Everything you need is available!

The Internet now offers home-based businesses the same tools for accounting, communication, and marketing that are used by multinational companies.

You can be a pro right from the start!

Tremendous resources are now available online, in business magazines, tapes, CD's, seminars, and through local self-help business groups.

There are people literally everywhere who are living the life of home-based business entrepreneurs that will be delighted to share their ideas and success stories!

There is no other avenue that allows you to stay completely in the driver's seat of your life like that of a home-based business.

Start **TODAY** to enjoy **ALL THE BENEFITS:**

- **Personal freedom**

Bette Graham was a typist who created a white paint to cover up mistakes on typed pages. She used it secretly for five years, but news spread. She sold it from her house for more than a decade, and even offered it to IBM, but was turned down. In 1979, she sold her Liquid Paper to Gillette Corporate for cool $47.5 million. Bette may have stumbled on a great idea, but she did an excellent job selling it to the world!

- **Reduction of stress**
- **Including your family**
- **Significant financial reward**
- **Increased competitive edge**
- **Greater productivity**
- **Tremendous tax advantages**

I know you are filled with desire for success, a willingness to grow, a thirst for knowledge, and possess a "won't quit attitude" or you wouldn't be reading this book.

At no time in history have the incredible opportunities for a home-based business been more available and desirable.

Know that the sky is truly the limit. You are free to chart your own course because you are in charge.

Selling Puts You in Charge

Imagine a company that started in the 1930s being hip, trendy, and attractive today!

How would you do that? How do you stay in charge?

In selling, you are able to do that. You adjust, change, and grow, which is exactly what salespeople do. The very nature of successful salespeople is the backbone that keeps a company on the cutting edge. The name of this "old" company that is perpetually a "new" company? Government Employees Insurance Company, or GEICO.

In 1984, Nedra Roney and her entrepreneurial-minded brother, Blake Roney, did some research and found a gap in the skin care industry that they thought they could fill. Doing more than a billion dollars in sales per year, Nu Skin has proven itself to the skin care industry, and proven the Roneys were right! They took charge and sales reflect that.

In the mid 1930s — ***right in the midst of the Great Depression*** — **Leo Goodwin** thought he found a way to increase sales in a way that minimized risk. The answer: sell auto insurance to federal employees and the top three grades of noncommissioned military officers.

By targeting this customer group, which he felt would consist of safe, conscientious, and employed drivers, he could provide car insurance at a lower price. The demographics of the group meant lower premiums and a steady profit.

He was right. **His creative imagination, combined with his ability to sell, mixed together for a great financial return!**

Leo's wife, **Lillian**, was a bookkeeper by profession and she took an active role in underwriting policies, setting rates, issuing policies, and marketing auto insurance to their target customers. By the end of 1936, their first year in operation, there were 3,700 policies in force and a total staff of 12 people.

The company continued to grow and in 1951, the legendary **Warren Buffett** took a train to Washington on a Saturday to learn more about GEICO. The office was closed, but the janitor directed him to **Lorimer Davidson**, an investment banker who worked to get new investors for GEICO.

Davidson, like **Leo Goodwin**, was a good salesman! **Warren Buffett** made his first purchase of GEICO stock.

In 1958, **Leo Goodwin** retired and **Davidson** was named successor. The 1960s were good years for GEICO: 1 millionth policyholder was

---

Charles P. Strite saw the problem: burned toast. He went to work to find an answer and in 1921 he patented his "Toastmaster." Immediately, he chose selling and with financial backing, started a company selling his toasters to the American population. By 1930, he was selling more than a million a year! He wanted to be in charge and selling was his ticket!

---

sold in 1964, net earnings doubled to $13 million in 1966, and GEICO opened a number of sales and service offices for walk-in customers and its first drive-in claims office.

Incredible selling by a company that no longer had its founder at the helm! That alone is a feat, but GEICO was not built on one person. It was built on selling a real service to people who needed it and could afford it.

In the early 1970s, both **Leo** and **Lillian Goodwin** passed away, and a few years later, it seemed the aggressive expansion was beginning to cost the company more than it expected. Wisely, GEICO strengthened its underwriting and reserving activities, which in turn helped build the company's reputation as a fiscally superior organization.

GEICO paused, learned, and improved. Exactly what salespeople do!

Then in 1976, **Warren Buffett** made a second purchase of GEICO stock, reported to total 1 million shares! That was a big boost to the company.

Business expanded slowly (the customer base now included the average person, not just government employees) but steadily throughout the 1980s. GEICO introduced 24-hour, 365-day telephone service for claims, sales, and service. The emphasis on customer service was exactly what customers needed. **Further great selling!**

In the 1990s came a new chairman, president, and CEO, and an increased advertising budget. GEICO was moving toward national visibility.

Dallin Larsen had worked in sales and marketing for many years and had helped expand other successful companies to various parts of the world, but he was not satisfied. "I had a dream of starting my own company," he says. Dallin wanted to be in charge. Today, his company, MonaVie, is experiencing rocket growth, and he only started in 2005!

It was at this point that **Warren Buffett** made his move. His Berkshire Hathaway investment firm bought out the remaining shares of GEICO's outstanding stock, and by 1996, GEICO was a subsidiary of one of the most profitable organizations in the country.

The result? National advertising that propelled GEICO to a whole new level! No doubt you've seen the GEICO Gecko TV commercials. The Gecko first appeared in 2000, and he quickly became an advertising icon. The GEICO Cavemen commercials followed a few years later, as did many other humorous, irrelevant, star-studded commercials.

The effect?

GEICO continues to grow, change, and expand. They have surpassed 8 million policyholders, assets are over $20 billion, they offer online services, and much, much more.

The company states that their growth will only be limited by the time it takes to hire knowledgeable associates committed to GEICO's way of thinking, which can be summed up in these words:

- excellent coverage
- low prices
- outstanding customer service

These ingredients are simple sales tools, which have enabled a 1930s company to be hip, trendy, and in demand today! **Without question, GEICO is in charge.**

When 5'7"Jean Nidetch was 38-years-old, she weighed 214 pounds and described herself as an "overweight housewife obsessed with eating cookies." In 1961, she combined a sensible diet with group support meetings ... and within a year, Jean had lost 72 pounds. The other women also had great results. Jean's entrepreneurial mind could see the unlimited business potential, and she took her Weight Watchers worldwide. Today, there are more than a million members who attend 29,000 meetings in 27 countries. Jean Nidetch can sell!

Stay In Charge

Chapter Seven:
Summary

1. **For many, the best way to take advantage of the opportunity that selling presents is to start with a home-based business.** A home-based business places you – and no one but you – completely in the driver's seat of your life!

2. **Success is entirely up to you.** Regardless of education level, social status, color, sex, age, or size, what is important is your burning desire to succeed and the perseverance to refuse to give up until you see your goals fully realized.

3. **The seven primary benefits of a home-based business are:** personal freedom, reduce your stress, include your family, significant financial reward, increase your competitive edge, greater productivity, and enjoy tax advantages.

4. **You can start a home-based business at any level.** It could be part time, full time, in your garage, or a spare room, with help or without, with minimum investment, and a minimum of obligations or risk.

5. **The very nature of successful salespeople** – the ability to adjust, change, and grow – **is the backbone that keeps a company on the cutting edge.**

All men's gains are a fruit of risk. As I see it, the biggest risk is hoping that you can succeed in life without being a master salesperson.

Chapter Eight

Real Questions and Real Answers

With Paul J. Meyer

Q: What am I thinking at this point?

A: I know what you are thinking. You are thinking about a guaranteed income. A consistent salary. A steady paycheck. But every salary has a floor, and if it has a floor, then it also has walls and a ceiling. *A salary limits your future. It limits your fortune. It limits your income potential. It limits your life.* And I know that is not what you want!

Q: Isn't selling a risky move?

A: You take a risk riding the bus, driving your car, and getting in the bathtub. You take risks going to work, riding in a

---

Lydia Jokonya worked for a bank in the capital city of Harare, Zimbabwe. She wanted more out of life and chose selling, becoming an SMI Distributor. She learned how to sell in an economy that is out of control. In one day she made a sale over $125,000! Lydia chose the opportunity that could take her to the top!

---

plane, and climbing a mountain. You must weigh the risks that you take, but consider this:

- **You can't possibly be better off staying in a small apartment when you could own your own home.**

- **You can't possibly be better off driving an old car when you could be driving a new car.**

- **You can't possibly be better off staying inside when you have never seen the ocean.**

- **You can't possibly be better off feeling restricted when you could be free.**

- **You can't possibly be better off living on one side of the tracks when you want to live on the other side.**

All men's gains are a fruit of risk. As I see it, the **biggest risk is hoping that you can succeed in life without being a master salesperson!**

Q: Do I need a college degree to succeed in sales?

A: If you want to sell in an area that requires a great deal of technical product knowledge, then a college degree may be necessary ... but no degree guarantees success in selling! I have found that it is easier to teach salespeople technical knowledge than it is to teach people how to sell. In other words, if you want to sell, then dive in. Don't let the lack of any degree keep you from pursuing your dreams.

Drayton McLane expanded his father's wholesale grocery business into a $19 billion enterprise. He went on to become the vice chairman of Wal-Mart and then owner of the Houston Astros. He is a sales leader and persuader personified.

Q: Why do some good salespeople fail despite their good education and sales knowledge of the products?

> **A: All successful people are motivated by end results**, and salespeople who fail are motivated by short-term results. In other words, let's say you decide that you are going to make $2,000 a week. As soon as your commissions fall below that figure, you will quit. If you only have short-range things in sight, then anything can stop you. An unkind word, an unexpected "no," an inconsiderate attitude, or anything that you are not happy with can stop you. On the other hand, if you have a long-range goal and are motivated by end result, you will overcome obstacles, attitudes, and circumstances. **Nothing can stop you!**

Q: What makes a salesperson succeed?

> **A:** It begins with a strong desire to be successful. You must set a goal and be determined to **stick with it**. The only guarantee lies within you.

Q: What can I do to prepare myself?

> **A:** The best way to prepare is to get out there and start selling. You can't stay in the harbor with sail neatly folded. You must set sail and go out into the waves and spray to bring back the cargoes of the world. Know-how comes from experience. Experience, in turn, comes from submitting yourself to obstacles, challenges, and situations. If you want to learn to close a deal, try it. If you make one less mistake every day, you are going to be a very good salesperson in a short amount of time.

Bill Clinton is smart, but his real talent is his ability to persuade and convince. He is a master salesman who went on to become President of the United States.

Q: How important is goal-setting in selling?

A: Goal-setting is incredibly important in selling. That is because an indefinite goal produces an indefinite result at best. You can't draw anything to you that your thoughts repel. Your thoughts repel anything they can't see, and they can't see anything you don't have down in black and white. Writing crystallizes thoughts, and thoughts motivate action. When you write down your goals, you begin the process of reaching your goals. Trust me. This works!

Q: Are there certain characteristics that all good sales-people possess?

A: Sure, they include: perseverance, self-reliance, self-confidence, the ability to be a starter, resilience, and the ability to get knocked down, and stand back up again. These characteristics are basic foundation blocks for success in any field where the major bucks are.

Q: What role does motivation play in selling?

A: Motivation is very important to success in selling. There really is no real motivation except personal motivation. Personal motivation is the development of inner strength, conscious willpower, overwhelming desire, and the determination to reach any goal you personally want to achieve. Successful salespeople do just that! They are self-motivated to achieve their own success.

Anne Mulcahy joined Xerox in 1976 as a lowly sales representative, but her superior sales skills began to push her to the top. Years later, she was elected President and COO (2000), CEO (2001), and Chairman (2002). Anne is a master saleswoman!

Q: How important is enthusiasm to selling?

A: *Enthusiasm is the most contagious personality quality there is.* It is impossible to project enthusiasm that is not real and have it be believable. You can only be lastingly and genuinely enthusiastic about something you are interested in, know about, and believe in. When you are enthusiastic about something, selling is downright easy!

Q: What if I don't have much self-confidence?

A: When you are actively engaged in doing something that is worthwhile, such as providing a service that is truly valuable to your customers, then there is no time for fear, insecurity, or lack of confidence. You can begin each day without giving mental recognition to the possibility of defeat because you are helping people, and helping yourself. You exude this confidence. It's in your handshake, your eyes, and your walk. And it comes easily when you believe in the product you are selling, whatever it might be.

Q: What is the most effective type of sales training?

A: The best sales training is always what you get when you are engaged in a face-to-face sales situation with a potential customer, and getting better and learning more from each presentation. Books and seminars can help, but hands-on activity is always going to be the best trainer. (I recommend Tom Hopkins www.tomhopkins.com for sales training.)

Charlie "Tremendous" Jones was the author and editor of nine books, including *Life is Tremendous* with more than 2,000,000 copies in print in 12 languages. At the young age of 23 he received awards for being a top insurance salesman. He continued to use his selling ability as a business owner, publisher, speaker, and best-selling author. Charlie was a master of the game of selling.

Q: How do you decide what sales company to join?

A: This question implies that you are ready to take action, which is great! I would begin by listing the companies, products, or tools that you are interested in selling. Then do a little research to see if the company is sound, solid, and based on principles that are agreeable. Follow that with financial questions: what is the compensation plan, potential for more income, residual income possibilities, etc. If that also is agreeable for you (and your spouse, if you are married), then find a local sales rep for this company and meet for lunch. Pick his or her brains for other important pieces of information. If you can, buy the product, membership, or service. Then dive in!

Q: Is there any other profession that offers the strategic opportunities of selling?

A: No! Once you're a master salesman, you can go anywhere you want, be anything you wish. More people in high positions in major companies began with selling than with anything else. Salespeople are the backbone of the free enterprise system. They are the backbone of the future!

Q: What about retirement?

A: *When you sell with the right opportunity, you have created future income called residual income.* Whether it's from commissions, real estate you purchased, businesses you created, stock dividends, or something else, you have stored

---

Born with a spinal disease, Debbie George knew that she would have to become an entrepreneur and start her own business. She wanted to make a living and make a difference and direct selling was her answer. Today, she enjoys a six-figure income and has the time and freedom to do what she wants to do. Only in selling could Debbie find the opportunity she wanted.

up wealth that will benefit you for years to come. And all the while you've traveled the world, called the shots, and picked where you wanted to live. In a sense, you've been retired since you chose the selling opportunity. Why would you want to stop!

Q: What impact do you have in people's lives?

A: More than you know! As a master salesperson, you are not only offering a valuable service or product, but you are also able to offer someone a better way of life. I've done it literally thousands of times. I have personally helped insecure people become self-confident, poor people become rich, and average people become top performers. Their lives were radically changed, to say the least. It is always an honor to be a part of that change, but change always comes about when people become master salespeople. It is invigorating to the depths of your soul!

Q: Does selling become a way of life?

A: Absolutely! Why would it change? You started selling with your first scream out of the womb. You have been selling your parents, siblings, neighbors, families, teachers, business partners, employers, employees, and others all your life. You just haven't given it the prominence that it deserves. Now you are considering choosing selling as a career. The best choice you will ever make! I have a hard

---

Ruth Handler saw an opportunity in the marketplace. She took the idea to her husband Elliot, a co-founder of the Mattel toy company. He was unenthusiastic about the idea, as were Mattel's directors. But Ruth kept on selling ... and the Barbie doll was born. Today it is estimated that over a billion Barbie dolls have been sold worldwide in over 150 countries, and Mattel claims that three Barbie dolls are sold every second!

---

time imagining the huge payoff that myself and my family would have missed if I had not chosen selling as a young man. I improved my 1 in 13 sales average (my first 9 months brought in $87 in sales) because I had stick-to-itiveness, persistence, and I could visualize the end result. Eventually the dam busted and there has been a cash flow to me and my family and our charitable foundations above and beyond what any of us could have imagined. Because I am so passionate about the return, I cannot help but tell others about it!

In 1977, two lifelong, ex-hippie friends completed a correspondence course on ice cream making from Penn State University. The next year, with a $12,000 investment, Ben Cohen and Jerry Greenfield opened an ice cream parlor in a renovated gas station in downtown Burlington, Vermont. The parlor quickly became popular in the local community because of their innovative flavors and ingredients. Ben and Jerry's ice cream was born because Ben and Jerry could sell!

Real Questions And Real Answers

Chapter Eight:
Summary

1. **Every consistent salary or guaranteed income has a floor.** If it has a floor, then it also has walls and a ceiling. A salary limits your future, fortune, income potential, and life. You must weigh the risks you take, but realize that all gains are a fruit of risk. The biggest risk is hoping that you can succeed in life without being a master salesperson!

2. **There is no college degree that guarantees success in selling.** It's easier to teach salespeople technical knowledge than it is to teach people how to see. Don't let the lack of any degree keep you from pursing your dreams.

3. **Salespeople who succeed are motivated by end results; salespeople who fail are motivated by short-term results.** With a long-range goal and motivation, you will overcome obstacles, negative attitudes, and circumstances. Being a top salesperson begins with a strong desire to be successful.

4. **The best way to prepare to be a salesperson is to get out there and start selling.** Know-how comes from experience. Experience, in turn, comes from submitting yourself to obstacles, challenges, and situations.

5. **Goal-setting is incredibly important in selling.** An indefinite goal produces an indefinite result at best. Writing crystallizes thoughts and thoughts motivate action. Write down your goals.

6. **All good salespeople possess certain characteristics that include:** perseverance, self-reliance, self-confidence, the

ability to be a self-starter, resilience, and the ability to get knocked down, and stand back up again.

7. **Motivation is very important to success in selling; there really is no real motivation except personal motivation.** Personal motivation is the development of inner strength, conscious willpower, overwhelming desire, and the determination to reach any goal you personally want to achieve.

8. **Enthusiasm and self-confidence are key attributes of successful salespeople.** These attributes come easily when you believe in the product you are selling, whatever that might be.

9. **The best sales training is always what you get when you are engaged in a face-to-face sales situation with a potential customer, and getting better and learning more from each presentation.** Books and seminars can help, but hands-on activity is always going to be the best trainer.

10. **To determine which sales organization to join, first list the companies, products, or tools that you are interested in selling.** Then do a little research to determine if the company is sound, based on principles that are agreeable. Look closely at key factors such as the compensation plan and residual income possibilities. If you like what you see, meet with the company's local sales representative to find out more.

11. **When you sell with the right opportunity, you have created future income called residual income.** Whether it's from commissions, real estate you purchased, businesses you created, or stock dividends, you have stored up wealth that will benefit you for years to come and in your retirement.

12. **As a master salesperson, you are not only offering a valuable service or product, but you are also able to offer someone a better way of life.** Change always comes about when people become master salespeople. Selling is invigorating – it becomes a way of life!

Selling is an option, choice,
and opportunity that comes fully
equipped with freedom,
potential, and fortune.
I've never found anything
else like it.

Conclusion

What To Do Next

... choose selling!

If you want the attributes of the master salespeople and want to become what they have become ... *choose selling*.

If you want to have the income that master salesperson enjoy ... *choose selling.*

If you have been downsized, "rightsized," terminated, or laid off ... *choose selling*.

If you are dissatisfied with your current income, not to mention your income potential ... *choose selling*.

If you are a female and you think you are limited, passed over, or that you've hit the glass ceiling ... *choose selling*.

If you are a college student trying to decide on a profession ... *choose selling*.

I get a 'high' from selling! And I want to sell you on the incredible profession, career, and occupation of selling. I want to sell you on what you can become as a result. If you could be anything, be a salesperson!

If you have been discriminated against because of your accent, education, color, race, or the side of the tracks you grew up on … *choose selling*.

If you have been overlooked one too many times or been relegated to a place in the business that gives you no hope of a future within the company … *choose selling.*

If you are tired of being told what to do, when to do it, how to do it, where to do it, and why to do it and you want to be free to be your own person … *choose selling.*

If you want to be paid what you are worth … *choose selling.*

If you dream of a bigger car, a nicer home, or even more children, but you can't see it happening on your current budget… *choose selling.*

If you feel like life is battleship gray and you long for the vibrant colors of a bright future … *choose selling.*

If you want to reach the top, and possibly be the CEO, president, or owner … *choose selling.*

Salespeople are the ones who write their own paychecks. There are no limitations! They have independence. They control their own time. They carve out their own destiny. They are the ones that companies want to hire. They are the ones that companies want to promote. And they are often the ones who end up leading the company!

For six years, I worked on writing one personal development program. Countless publishers turned me down, so I produced and sold it myself. Sales of that one single program topped $700 million and my personal commissions were over $100 million. In today's dollars, that would be over $500,000,000. I pursued my own dream by selling.

You cannot find any other profession that makes these claims!

When you choose selling, you make your own music, you sell your own music, and you dance to your own music.

When you choose selling, you become the president and chairman of your own company … and all the company shares are yours!

When you choose selling, you package yourself each day, and sell that package to your prospects.

My oldest son, Jim, sells! He was one of Texas' most successful litigation lawyers. He knew the law, but his success came from selling jurors.

My middle son, Larry, sells! He was the #1 selling franchise many years ago for one of my companies. Now he is a leading developer of real estate and is a master at buying and selling property.

My youngest son, Billy, sells! He sells people to come to his racetrack, the Texas Motorplex. He sells people on building restoration and he buys and sells private jets.

My son-in-law, Randy Slechta, sells! He sells people on selling for his family's company, Leadership Management International, which sells leadership programs in 60 countries and 24 languages.

My other son-in-law, Kevin Rhea, sells! He sells people on selling and has built the #1 agency in North America selling legal insurance for Pre-Paid Legal Services, Inc.

And because they all mastered selling, they all make millions and are multi-millionaires today. How? They all chose selling, and so can you!

When you choose selling, you decide what you want out of life, knowing that you have what it takes to accomplish it.

When you choose selling, you have something that will stir your blood.

When you choose selling, you live on top of a hill where the air is fresh and the wind is strong … instead of living at the bottom of the valley where life is stale and the winds of change seldom blow.

When you choose selling, you walk in the Milky Way, you see the moon, and you can touch the stars.

When you choose selling, you have something that will stir your blood.

As you can see, or maybe you already know, selling is by far the greatest opportunity in the world! Selling is a job of hope.

Selling is an opportunity to achieve your dreams.

Selling has no ceilings of any kind.

Selling is the opportunity to develop more of your full potential.

Selling sets you free!

Selling can lift you out of a life of mediocrity.

Selling can provide you with the income of the rich and famous.

Selling is a lifetime of opportunity. It never stops. It is like a spring that continues to produce fresh water, day in and day out. If you want a life of continuous opportunity, there is no question: choose selling!

Selling can give you opportunities that have been out of reach.

Selling opens the gate to greener pastures.

Selling has the power to fan the smallest flame into a blazing fire.

Selling gives you an incredible chance to reach out and accomplish your wildest dreams.

Choose selling.

When I was 27, I was a millionaire. That would be over $12 million in today's dollars. Since then, I have made hundreds of millions in sales and in commissions, all of which I attribute to becoming a master salesman. Could I have done this in a field other than selling? I doubt it. I never finished grammar school or high school, and only spent six weeks in college. Remember, when you choose selling, the road is open, the ladder is up, and the sky is the limit!

Tools of the Trade

Now That You've Chosen Selling

*... here are very practical tools to help
you accomplish your goals!*

I'm a salesman ... *let me sell you on something*.

Let me sell you on the **one thing** that has the power to catapult you
to success beyond your wildest dreams!

Let me sell you on the "**secret**" that has enabled the poor and the weak
to become rich and powerful.

Are you ready for it?

Here it is: **<u>making an investment in yourself.</u>**

How?

FIRST, invest in the area of selling.

By choosing selling, you have embarked on the most incredible of
journeys! It is a life-long learning process that will keep you up at
nights, full of vision and excitement, and make you bounce out of bed
before the alarm clock rings!

One requirement is that you get your Master's Degree in Selling, which will be:

- Self-given
- Self-earned
- Self-mastered
- Self-deserved
- Self-attained

Attend sales trainings, read sales books, and listen to as much sales training as you can … more than once. Absorb the principles and put them into practice.

The master ability to sell makes for a potent combination!

I would also recommend these sales-training tools:

Books:
>*How to Win Friends & Influence People* – Dale Carnegie
>*Sell Yourself Rich* – Mark Victor Hansen
>*How to Master the Art of Selling* – Tom Hopkins
>*Low Profile Selling* – Tom Hopkins
>*The Greatest Salesman in the World* – Og Mandino
>*Prospecting Rules* – Russ McNeil
>*A Fortune to Share* – Paul J. Meyer
>*The Absolute Best Way in the World for Women to Make Money* – Lorna Rasmussen
>*The Referral of a Lifetime* – Tim Templeton
>*Integrity Selling* – Ron Willingham
>*Zig Ziglar's Secrets of Closing the Sale* – Zig Ziglar

CDs:
>*Enthusiasm Sells* – Paul J. Meyer
>*How to Close Sales and When* – Paul J. Meyer
>*How to Get More Sales Interviews* – Paul J. Meyer
>*How to Prospect Your Way to Millions* – Paul J. Meyer
>*How to Turn Objections Into Sales* – Paul J. Meyer
>*Qualities of Successful Sales Professionals* – Paul J. Meyer
>*The Psychology of Selling* – Brian Tracy

Magazines & Websites:

www.leaderexcel.com
www.pauljmeyer.com
www.sellingpower.com
www.tomhopkins.com

Associations:

Direct Selling Association (The Direct Selling Association (DSA) is the national trade association of the leading firms that manufacture and distribute goods and services sold directly to consumers.) www.dsa.org

National Association of Sales Professionals (Helping salespeople advance their career status & security; located in Scottsdale, Arizona.) www.nasp.com

Strategic Account Management Association (International association dedicated to promoting the concept of customer-supplier partnering. Customers are managers and executives charged with leading their company's strategic sales initiatives.) www.strategicaccounts.org

National Field Selling Association (Non-profit trade association promoting & inspiring professional excellence in the direct selling industry in the United States.) www.nfsa.com

SECOND, invest in the area of personal development.

I met the legendary W. Clement Stone in 1957 and we had many discussions about personal development over the next 50 years. He was a director of my company when we first met, but we became fast friends. He introduced me to many other movers and shakers in the personal development industry.

When I founded Success Motivation Institute in 1960, and many other companies since then, I have used personal development as a tool to equip and train every salesperson in my company.

As a result, they became better, smarter, people who made even more money as a result of what happened to them on the inside. Literally, hundreds of people who worked for me — who became masters of selling and masters of personal development — went on to launch their own businesses.

I even met a businessman who unashamedly said, "I'm moving my business to your town and I plan to hire as many people as I can from your companies." What he was saying was that he wanted people in his companies who were personally developed.

While you are working to reach your full potential through mastering selling and working on personal development, here is a list of resources that you ought to consider investing in:

Books:

As a Man Thinketh – James Allen
The One-Minute Entrepreneur – Ken Blanchard and Don Hutson
The One-Minute Manager – Ken Blanchard and Spencer Johnson
Gung Ho! – Ken Blanchard and Sheldon Bowles
The Tripping Point in Leadership, – David Byrd
Richest Man in Babylon – George S. Clason
Acres of Diamonds – Russell H. Conwell
The Seven Habits of Highly Effective People – Stephen R. Covey
Life Is Tremendous – Charlie "T" Jones
The Greatest Salesman in the World – Og Mandino
Developing the Leader Within You – John Maxwell
24 Keys that Bring Complete Success – Paul J. Meyer
5 Pillars of Leadership – Paul J. Meyer and Randy Slechta
Power of Positive Thinking – Norman Vincent Peale
The Millionaire Next Door – Thomas J. Stanley
The Success System that Never Fails – W. Clement Stone
The Psychology of Winning – Denis Waitley
The Purpose Driven Life – Rick Warren
See you at the Top – Zig Ziglar

CDs:

A Fortune to Share – Paul J. Meyer (CD & DVD)
Positive Expectancy to Win – Paul J. Meyer

The Courage to Succeed – Paul J. Meyer
Never, Never, Never Give Up! – Paul J. Meyer
Self-Motivation for Winners – Paul J. Meyer
If You Don't Have Discipline, You Don't Have Anything –
Paul J. Meyer
Harness the Power of Your Attitude – Paul J. Meyer
The Awesome Power of Negative Thinking – Paul J. Meyer
The Seeds of Greatness – Denis Waitley

Sales and Personal Development Programs:
Success Motivation Institute programs: 254-776-9967
(www.success-motivation.com)

THIRD, track your efforts.

I have always said that if you can measure it, you can manage it. What's more, if you track your efforts, you know exactly where you succeeded and where you need to improve.

The successes propel you forward, even faster. And the areas that you need to improve, you do just that. Win-win!

Many years ago, I worked with my salespeople to track their efforts, to keep them on target, and to help them reach their sales goals. The result was the MyTyme Success Planner.

It is, without question, one of the best tools for salespeople. It helps track efforts, encourages accountability, and helps you focus on reaching your sales goals. Patrick Shaw, a top salesman in one direct marketing company has trained his top salespeople to ... use the MyTyme Success Planner with their teams, and the results have been staggering! To order, simply call toll free: 888-469-8963.

Each MyTyme Success Planner is custom-built, beginning with the month that you start. You buy 12-month calendar inserts and keep the rest of your Success Planner. It becomes a living, breathing entity that works to increase your success, every step of the way!

FOURTH, dive in and do it.

The last part is the best part. This is your chance to dive in, to swim in the ocean of limitless potential, to cement into your heart and mind what you have learned.

This is the part that puts money in your pocket.

This is the part where you go out and make the sale!

This is the part where you don't look back. You have chosen selling, and the world awaits you!

SELLING is
unequivocally,
indisputably,
undeniably,
irrefutably,
obviously,
definitely,
plainly,
and without question
THE WORLD'S GREATEST OPPORTUNITY!

Index of Companies

Index of People

ORDER FORM:

_____Library   copies X $_____ = $ _____

_____Library   copies X $_____ = $ _____

_____Library   copies X $_____ = $ _____

_____Library   copies X $_____ = $ _____

Product Total $ _____

S/H $9/library set $ _____

Sales Tax (TX residents only) 8.25% $ _____

Email customer service for international orders

Name:_____ Title:_____

Organization:_____

Shipping Address:_____

City:_____ State:_____ ZIP:_____

Phone: _____ Fax:_____

E-Mail: _____

Charge Your Order:

☐ MasterCard ☐ VISA ☐ AMERICAN EXPRESS ☐ DISCOVER

CC#: _____ Exp date:_____

☐ Check Enclosed (Payable to PJM Resources)

Paul J. Meyer Resources
PO Box 7411
Waco, TX 76714
Fax: 254-751-0475

Email: <u>ServiceTeam2@theleadingedgepublishing.com</u>

Leadership Excellence

Celebrating 25 Years of Excellence